Communication Craft

Simple Ways to Improve Your Personal and Professional Relationships

Christian Gilbert

Michi Press

Copyright © 2022 Christian Gilbert

All rights reserved. No part of this publication may be reproduced, distributed, or transmitted in any form or by any means, including photocopying, recording, or other electronic or mechanical methods, without the prior written permission of the publisher, except in the case of brief quotations embodied in critical reviews and certain other noncommercial uses permitted by copyright law.

ISBN: 979-8-9858648-0-9 (Paperback)
ISBN: 979-8-9858648-1-6 (Hardcover)
ISBN: 979-8-9858648-2-3 (eBook)

For more information about special discounts available for bulk purchases, sales promotions, fundraising, educational needs, or for permissions requests, please write to the author at info@christiangilbert.com.

Printed by Michi Press, in the United States of America.
First Edition: June 2022
Author's website: www.ChristianGilbert.com

Contents

Introduction	1
PART I: Interpersonal Communication	7
1. Be Understood	9
Noise	
Memetics	
2. Avoid Misunderstanding	31
Gricean Maxims	
Speech Acts	
Biases & Fallacies	
3. Improve Your Relationships	63
Attraction	
Love Styles	
Satisfaction & Stability	
The Four Horsemen	
4. Learn the Truth About Lie-Detection	89
Information Manipulation	
Deception Detection	
5. Read People	107
Kinesics	
Oculesics	

  Proxemics
  Haptics
  Vocalics
  Environments
  Chronemics
  Olfactics

PART II: Public Discourse   139

6. Talk About What's True   147
  Solipsism: What do we really know?
  Bayesian Inference: How do we choose what to believe?
  Falsifiability: What kind of evidence can we use?
  The Burden of Proof: Where do we get evidence?
  Occam's Razor: How do we explain our evidence?
  The CRAAP Test: How can you fact-check in your own life?

7. Talk About What's Good   177
  Utilitarianism
  Deontology
  Practical vs. Principle
  Polarization
  Moral Foundations Theory
  The Monkeysphere

PART III: Public Speaking   209

8. Prepare Exceptional Presentations   211
  GREAT Points TOO
  GREAT
  Points
  TOO

Supporting Materials

9. Build Your Confidence — 241
   Subconscious Self-Talk for Success
   The 10 Thoughts Stealing Your Confidence

Conclusion — 263

Book Recommendations — 267

If You Enjoyed This Book... — 272

Acknowledgements — 275

Notes — 277

About the Author — 293

Introduction

If you were one of the first people on Mars, what would be the hardest part of your job? In 2016, a team of researchers confined on the Big Island of Hawai'i were released. They had spent one year in isolation with each other to simulate what life might be like on Mars. For frontiers of human achievement, putting humans on the surface of Mars is probably the single greatest feat humans can accomplish right now, a major tick on humanity's bucket list.

One of the researchers released from isolation was Christiane Heinicke, who was interviewed on NPR.[1] The interviewer asked what had been the most difficult part of the last year, and I was anxious for her answer. Maybe the hardest part was managing their oxygen supply. Maybe it was recycling their water to keep it clean. Maybe it was growing their own food in hydroponic labs. She didn't mention any of those situations.

It was *getting along* with people. If there was ever a conflict, you couldn't storm out of the room and slam the door behind you because opening doors meant introducing Martian atmosphere into your oxygenated, pressurized environment and everyone would die. You couldn't just block someone like you can on social media. No, you were stuck together in the same dome for a year. If there was a conflict, you had to work it out. Can you imagine what that would be like in your own life today? What if you had to address every little conflict that arose head on, and you had no choice but to see it through? What if you had to keep the peace with the people around you because your lives depended on it?

Even at the frontier of human achievement, taking our first steps towards another planet, the most difficult part of the mission wasn't an issue of engineering, mathematics, physics, or chemistry, but communication.

In graduate school, I learned about a unique field of communication research: bad news. Now, when we think about academically rigorous jobs, many of us might think of doctors. Doctors must go through hours of training, studying anatomy, physiology, treatments, symptoms, and diagnoses. Medicine is a very difficult subject that requires expertise in microbiology, neurology, pharmacology, and all kinds of other scary sounding -ologies. But it turns out one of the most difficult problems facing modern-day doctors wasn't diagnosing strange symptoms or understanding certain biological ailments. It was delivering bad news.

I had never thought about that before. Imagine being a doctor and working with a family for years, maybe you got a chance to see your patient become a parent. You got a chance to see their child grow up to graduate high school. You were there with this family for all those years. Then one day, you face your patient with news that they only have three months to live. Can you imagine what that would be like? With all the preparation, schooling, studying, and expertise, it's extremely difficult to prepare oneself for that kind of experience. Research has found that some doctors struggled to communicate bad news effectively.[2] Some doctors would put it off until they found the right way to tell the patient, costing the patient valuable time. Sometimes doctors would deliver the news but in a way that was vague or equivocal, trying to lighten the burden of the news. Sometimes they would delegate delivering the news to someone else.

In one of the most academically rigorous careers one can imagine, involving some of the most complex subject matters one could study, one of the most difficult aspects of the job wasn't diagnosing strange symptoms or pharmacology—it was communication.

If we can improve our communication, we can improve just about everything else. Improving a seemingly small set of skills will yield a great number of improvements in your life. Whatever your background, whatever your field, whatever your interests, you can see a tremendous impact in your professional and personal life if you are able to improve your communication skills.

This book will help you craft your own communication by improving three big areas of your life. Part I covers *interpersonal communication*, the one-to-one interactions wherein we need to be understood (Chapter 1), avoid creating misunderstandings or misunderstanding others (Chapter 2), and have happy relationships in dating and marriage (Chapter 3). We'll also discuss some fun things like lie-detection (Chapter 4) and body language (Chapter 5).

In Part II, we will dive into the messy subject of *public discourse*. The world is replete with conspiracy theories, political tensions, and dinner table disputes we'd all much rather avoid, but know we'd somehow like to be prepared for, nonetheless. This part of the book will arm you with basic principles to engage in all sorts of disagreements about what's true (Chapter 6) and what's good (Chapter 7) with a solid foothold to emerge on the other side with equanimity and your relationships intact.

Finally, Part III tackles the communication skill most of us would love to avoid entirely: *public speaking*. At various points in your life, you will inevitably be called upon to present. If you are already a comfortable presenter—great! You will get the tools and techniques to refine your raw talent to a fine point (Chapter 8). If you are not at all comfortable with presenting—great! You will see how dissecting the techniques of the pros makes it all become extremely accessible. You can direct your self-talk away from nervousness and toward confidence (Chapter 9). You do not need to be born a skilled speaker to be a skilled speaker.

You can read through everything from start to finish or you can choose to jump around from section to section as you see fit. If the book is helpful to you, it is doing its job.

Before diving in, we should distinguish between methods and principles. *Methods* are specific actions you take to achieve a certain result; *principles* are larger governing rules from which we can derive methods. For example, a method for teaching your dog to sit might involve waiting for your dog to sit, saying the word "sit" as it does, and immediately giving the dog a treat. The underlying principle is that *what gets reinforced gets repeated*. The specific *method* will only work for getting a dog to sit, but the broader *principle* can be used to teach a dolphin to flip, a child to stop whining, or a husband to take out the trash.[3]

This book largely concerns itself with communication principles which can be applied to all different aspects of life. You will need to do a bit of thinking for how to specifically apply these principles in your relationships to derive the greatest benefit, but I thought that a book which prioritized principles over methods would ultimately give you the most use for the most situations.

That said, I don't want you to do all the work. At the end of each chapter, I include a list of "10 Tips" on the chapter's topic which offers specific, actionable ways to use the principles we just covered. Of course, the lists will not include every possible way to apply the concepts, but they will be tangible takeaways you can use immediately. While you could just skip ahead to the end of each chapter for the lists, many of the tips will not make much sense without understanding the concepts unpacked within the chapter. For example, the term "meme activation potential" is probably gibberish to you right now, but after you read Chapter 1, meme activation potential and its uses in our 10 Tips list will bring clarity to every conversation you have.

PART I: Interpersonal Communication

Chapter 1

Be Understood

"If you understood everything I say, you'd be me!"
— Miles Davis

How do we understand each other? It's a remarkable thing when you think about it. Ideas from one mind can appear in another mind. It's like magic. We do this so often without thinking, it's easy to take for granted. But if we want to avoid the frustration of being misunderstood, then we need to shine a light on this process to understand how it works.

When it comes to how communication works there are a couple of different models we can consider: the sender-receiver model and memetics. Let's start with the sender-receiver model.[4] We cannot just think a thought and have it appear in someone's mind. We can't even "send" a person our thoughts. The best we can do is send a *representation* of our thoughts. A sender, or the encoder, takes the meaning in their head and encodes it using signs and symbols while the receiver decodes the message. In this case, the encoder uses language to send a message through a channel, such as the spoken word or a text message.

Decoding the message entails unpacking the original meaning from the encoder. It's like I sent you a puzzle box that could be solved with a cypher. Assuming you know the same signs and symbols that I use (in this case, speaking or reading English), you successfully unpack my puzzle box by decoding the cypher. Voila! You have the meaning that I originally had in mind.

If you wanted to respond, you then take your own meaning and ideas, encode them with signs and symbols, and send them to me using a feedback channel. Then I would become the decoder and have to unpack the message and on and on it goes. It's a straightforward concept: senders and receivers sending words and messages to each other. However, the part that's less straightforward (and easy to miss) is the potential *noise* that's interfering with the model. Noise is everywhere. Not just the sounds we hear through our ears, but many other kinds of noise too.

Noise

For our purposes, we can define noise as anything that interferes with the flow of communication by blocking the symbols being sent or received. It could be anything in the minds of the encoders and decoders that might prevent them from properly encoding or decoding messages. So, if you can identify different types of noise to get around them, you can dramatically improve your interactions with other people. Here are four different types of noise you can start to identify in your interactions with people.

The first type of noise is **Environmental Noise**. This is what we probably tend to think of whenever we hear the word noise. You might think of an ambulance driving by, a loud car honking, or kids screaming or crying. While those are all types of noise, environmental noise includes anything that literally obstructs communication, such as speaking with someone over a video call but then your internet cuts out.

A poor signal interferes with communication. Maybe you're trying to have a conversation with somebody but there's a big brick wall between you. It's a silly way to talk to somebody but you probably could if you really had to. You could yell really loudly or knock on the bricks in a series of taps or rhythms in an attempt to communicate. You could still interact. It'd be possible but difficult. That's because the brick wall is noise, or the dropped internet signal is noise. Once we're aware of environmental noise, it's usually pretty easy to get around. You can reconnect your modem or wait until the loud ambulance passes by. But the next three types of noise are especially sinister because of how easy they are to miss.

The second type of noise is **Physical Noise**. Physical noises are not barriers of communication like environmental noise but are the physical things around us that distract us from our conversation. While you're walking and talking with a friend, maybe you smell something sweet like cookies, and you interrupt your friend with "Ohmigosh that smells so good!" Maybe it's a bad smell, and you stop the conversation by asking, "What smells so bad?" Physical noise can also be visual distractions or auditory distractions. Over coffee with a friend, you see an attractive person across from you and can't stop staring at them. Or instead, maybe you hear your favorite song come on the radio in the coffee shop and you can't help but hum to it.

The third type of noise is **Psychological Noise**. Now, psychological noise takes place purely in the minds of the speakers and listeners—our thoughts, feelings, and attitudes that might get in the way of effectively encoding or decoding messages. Remember being a young and angsty teenager with a crush? Maybe you're off eating lunch at school one day when suddenly, the cutie from calculus walks by and they look us in the eye for the first time. Time freezes, our heart stops and then, miracle of miracles, they say, "Hi."

Now our mind is racing. We're thinking, *"What do I say? They never spoke to me before. Now they know that I'm real, this is my chance. I'd better not blow it. Do I say hi? Do I play it cool? What's cool? Just be yourself. What is yourself? How do you be that on purpose?!"* Before you know it, your crush goes, "Okay, well, see you" and walks away. That moment where you froze? That's psychological noise—we had all this turmoil going on in our heads. Our minds were racing to figure out what to say or what to do. Just the act of thinking a million miles an hour was enough to interfere with our communication. That's exactly what psychological noise is. This psychological noise prevented us from properly encoding a message in the first place.

Nervousness isn't the only form of psychological noise. Here's something we do all the time in arguments without realizing it. You ever notice how when you're in an argument with someone, you're usually not really *listening* closely so much as you are *getting ready to respond?* We will latch on to a key idea from the other person and start dismantling it in our minds. We find a dozen ways their idea is wrong and then we wait for our opening when we can jump in and end the argument with our airtight logic.

That's psychological noise. Ironically, if we were to spend more time listening than preparing, we may actually have an easier time resolving the conflict. We might hear a key point of agreement we initially missed—an entry point to changing that person's mind. We might also hear something that convinces us *we* were in the wrong.

The fourth type of noise is **Semantic Noise**. Semantics has to do with meaning. This is any kind of noise that is based on symbols with multiple meanings, symbols that can be decoded in multiple ways. The meaning of what someone says becomes obscured or made ambiguous because the words they're using have multiple meanings. Now, this happens all the time because lots of words have multiple meanings and because language is always changing.

Think about the word *tweet*. I remember that if someone said they heard a tweet, you'd think, oh, that's nice, they heard a bird. But now if someone asks, "Did you hear about that tweet," we all think, "Ugh, what did that idiot celebrity do now?" It's because tweet means something very, very different. The English language is always changing. There used to be a time when you could honestly and innocently invite a friend over to watch Netflix and just chill. But the expression "Netflix and chill" has evolved into something a little bit different than just watching movies and hanging out.

This is why scientific words sound really fancy (even though they're not), whether it be the scientific names of animals, plants, medicines, or planets. It's kind of like a bunch of third graders just came in and named things with whatever came to mind. Don't take my word for it. Maybe you've heard of the corpse flower, which is a giant plant that blooms anywhere between every two to three years to once every seven years. Whenever it blooms, it smells like death, like a rotting body. It's rare and gross. So, naturally whenever it happens, everybody wants to check it out. Whenever it starts to bloom, it makes the local news. Once, my wife and I went over to Foster Botanical Garden in Honolulu, and we got the chance to learn the actual scientific name of the plant: *Amorphophallus titanum*.

That's some fancy, highfalutin science-speak, right? Not exactly. In science, researchers will name things in languages like ancient Greek and Latin because those languages aren't changing like modern languages do. The scientific names are universal, meaning everyone knows what they refer to, irrespective of what language they speak. The name today will mean the same thing 100 years from now. The name avoids semantic noise.

If you break down "*Amorphophallus titanum*" and look at its composite parts, you can see why they used that name. *Amorpho* from Greek—literally, without shape or form. Amorphous is a way to call something ugly. *Phallus*, also from Greek (via Latin)—penis. How about the last one? You can probably guess what *titanum* means. Large. So, *Amorphophallus titanum*? You guessed it—"Big ugly dick." That's the name of the plant now and shall be forever and ever. To someone who isn't familiar with ancient Latin and Greek, the name may sound fancy, but once you decode the message, its true meaning becomes clear.

Science is filled with silly names like this. The scientific name of the common domestic dog we're all familiar with is *Canis familiaris*. Sounds fancy? It's not. It literally means "friendly dog." Maybe you've heard of the great white shark, *Carcharodon carcharias*. Sounds fancy right? Nope. It means "shark-toothed shark." What about T-Rex, short for *Tyrannosaurus rex*. It means "tyrant lizard king" because it looks like a big, mean lizard. All these fancy-sounding scientific names are an effort to avoid semantic noise over generations of scientific research.

To summarize: there are four overarching categories of noise. If you have the ability to spot these types of interference, you can then work around them. Environmental noise literally obstructs communication. It could be an ambulance, a brick wall, or a dropped phone signal. Physical noise is external distraction that pulls away the attention of the communicators, like a cute dog or a car crash. Psychological noise takes place in the minds of the communicators, like being distracted, or having feelings, emotions, or prejudices. Finally, we have semantic noise, which occurs when meaning is obscured because symbols can be decoded in multiple ways, such as words with multiple meanings.

Hopefully, it feels like you have a bit more ammunition to start combating all the things that can confound your communication with other people. You can identify relevant problems and address them to improve your interactions. But what's actually happening in the minds of communicators, and how do you have the ability to control minds? For that, we'll need to talk about memetics.

Memetics

Let's talk about memes. Memes come from a field of work called memetics.[5] When we think of a meme, we probably think about funny internet pictures and funny looking texts. However, internet memes are not actually the origin of memes. Memetics is the study of ideas, or memes, and the ways in which ideas spread from person to person.

There are three overarching concepts in the field of memetics. If you can wrap your head around these three concepts, you'll have a deep grasp of how people interact with each other, something we very much take for granted without understanding why these interactions work or don't work.

Memes

The first of these three big concepts is the meme. To be clear, a meme is not just a picture of a cat with bold-face white font across the image. A meme is a *unit of meaning*. What's that?

Think about it like this: in your head you have a concept for "sandwich." You can see a sandwich. You can smell it. Maybe you like sandwiches, maybe you don't (but you should). Maybe you have memories making them with your uncle and auntie before you went to the park. Everything in your head related to sandwiches—your memories, your likes, your dislikes, definitions, imagery, colors, smells, everything that is sandwich in one package—that's a unit of meaning, a meme.

You have a meme for dogs, for love, for fear, for friendship, and anything you have a vague understanding of. Everything that is sandwich and is distinctly *not* robotics, or tabletop games, or taxes, or epidemiology, or stargazing is part of the meme. It's sandwich as one unit, as one *meme*.

Memes as a concept actually got started in biology because memetics studied how ideas spread from person to person. Richard Dawkins, an evolutionary biologist, coined the term because he noticed how ideas live in us, spreading from person to person, much like organisms spread from place to place.[6]

Successful animals, living organisms, will do two things exceptionally well. First, they will reproduce well. In the case of a fish, the animal lays a thousand eggs in the hopes that one or two of them will survive. Or creatures can go the other way. Humans have maybe one or two kids at a time, but we pay very close attention to them. We don't just ignore them like fish ignore their eggs. Our one or two offspring at a time will have a very high likelihood of surviving.

Secondly, successful organisms defend and protect themselves to keep from dying as best they can. Maybe that means growing a shell like a turtle does to protect itself from predators. Maybe it means growing spiky quills like a porcupine does in order to scare away predators. Or maybe it means being able to run really fast in quick bursts like a rabbit, or growing a strong immune system to fight off bacteria, diseases, and viruses.

These are the two things successful organisms do well. They reproduce and they protect. They have **spreading power** and **staying power**. As it turns out, ideas that are really successful will do the same things too, something that Richard Dawkins and other biologists noticed. Successful ideas are good at spreading from person to person, replicating and protecting themselves. In the same way animals who don't meet these reproductive or protective conditions don't survive, memes that don't reproduce or protect themselves will die off pretty quickly.

Highly "memetic" ideas encourage being spread and are more resistant to extinction. They have spreading power and staying power. For example, at some point in your life you've probably run into a dumb chain email, the kind where it says something like "share this email with 30 friends in the next five minutes otherwise the frog queen will crawl out of your toilet and slap you across the face." You know the sort.

The email does two things pretty well. First, it replicates, telling the reader to share this email with 30 friends in the next five minutes. Spreading power. Second, it defends itself by including punishment for not being spread. You don't want punishment. Staying power.

Here's another silly example. If you haven't heard of this one yet, you're never going to stop thinking about it, and you'll always resent this book for introducing you to..."The Game."

The way The Game works is you must not think about The Game. The moment you think about The Game, you've lost, and you must announce out loud that you've lost. Right now, you are losing The Game. I just lost, and I lost again, and so did you because we're both thinking about The Game. Up until this point in your life, if you've never heard of The Game, you've been winning because you never thought about it, so you've been doing a really good job. But now you've lost because you're thinking about it. Sorry about that.

Now, this is a highly memetic idea. It has the ability to spread exceptionally well. Someone will just be sitting around, maybe with a group of friends, and they just go, "Aagh, I lost," which of course makes everyone else ask, "What do you mean?" The first person has to explain what The Game is, and now everybody else is part of The Game. The Game can go on for years and years and years, replicating and defending itself because the rules include announcing when you lose out loud. That's an annoying example of a highly memetic idea.

What are some real-world memetic ideas? Many cultural, political, and religious ideas are highly memetic and spread prolifically. Some of the oldest and most successful religions on earth have terrific spreading power and staying power. The big three monotheistic faiths of Christianity, Judaism, and Islam certainly do. You might see themes of spreading and sharing the message, like proselytization or saving others. This might be something along the lines of "To save one soul is to have saved all of humanity." Spreading power.

These faiths are also good at defending themselves. They often promote marrying within the faith. If someone doubts the religion, that might be classified as temptation or sinful. If an individual takes it upon themselves to leave, that is also considered morally wrong. It's a built-in punishment. Staying power.

In that sense, these messages survive exceptionally well. It makes sense, all things considered. Consider how short-lived a faith might be if its central tenets were "Keep this to yourself" and "We're probably wrong."

Right now, you have a whole bunch of memes in your head. Memes for things like sandwich or friendship. Memes for things like The Game (we both just lost). Memes for things like *Amorphophallus titanum*, for cameras, for stars. What does any of this have to do with communication? Once you get comfortable with memes, we can discuss how memes are the way you mind control your friends.

Stimuli

Here's our second concept: a stimulus. For our purposes, a stimulus is any kind of sensory input that activates one of your five senses. Stimulus is singular, stimuli are multiple. One stimulus, many stimuli. Sounds are auditory stimuli, objects you see are visual stimuli, stuff you touch are tactile stimuli, and things you smell or taste are olfactory stimuli.

Why are stimuli important? Because memes and stimuli become intertwined as you grow up. Over the years, you start to associate different memes with specific stimuli. As soon as you're presented with a stimulus, a meme is activated. I'll give you an example:

Don't think of a black cat.

As soon as you read that, you think of a black cat. A few readers who are feeling especially sassy right now might insist they are thinking about something else, like a purple elephant with polka dots. That's fine, but even then, you still first think of a black cat before defiantly thinking of something else. Why do you automatically think of a black cat? According to the sender-receiver model, you should understand those words are a prohibition. This is where we begin to see the limitations of this model.

The sender-receiver model is not very accurate for describing how communication actually works. It's useful because it gives us terminology, like senders and receivers, to explain communication in basic terms, but they're not always accurate. If it were, once you decoded "Don't think of a black cat," you just wouldn't do it. But that's not what happened. You did think of a black cat. You didn't do it because you were defying the prohibition but because you couldn't help it. The words *black cat* made you think of a black cat.

Here's where memetics comes into play. In your head, you have a meme for a cat. You have a meme for the color black. You've got memes for thinking and memes for prohibition such as "don't." Over time, as you've grown up, you've come to associate these memes with different stimuli.

Say you and I are face-to-face. You aren't reading my words, you're hearing my voice (I'm presenting you with audible stimuli). Is there a noise I can make that's going to make you think of a cat? Maybe meowing. Imagine I did meow at you. The meow in and of itself is not a word. It's a noise. The meow sound activates the meme of a cat, but meow isn't a word.

Is there another noise I can make at you? I can also make this noise: "cat." The noise "cat" activates your meme for a cat. You might say that "cat" is a word, not a noise. But not really. When we communicate with each other we're making predictions about stimuli we've associated with memes so we can convey those stimuli to the other person, which will activate the memes associated with the received stimuli.

Imagine, for a moment, that you are about to undergo brain surgery. You are asked if you are willing to participate in some research. The research will be conducted while you are conscious and your skull is open. This will be done so people can see your brain (because the ability to study a living, awake brain is a rare opportunity). Suppose you agree. The top of your skull is moved aside for the duration of the experiment. While the brain is exposed, a researcher comes over with a little electrical prod thingy, hovers over one part of your brain, and with a light zap, touches it to your brain. You smack your lips. You taste oranges. The researcher scribbles something onto a clipboard.

The experience, the meme, of tasting oranges is locked away in your mind. Occasionally, we're able to activate those memes, those experiences, with a little prod. If any part of this thought experiment gives you the heebie-jeebies, that makes sense. It's a little heebie-jeebie thinking that ideas and experiences can be activated in our brains so automatically without our consent. But what if I told you this happens to you every day?

Meme Activation Potential

What if you had the ability to reach through someone's ears, into their brain, and automatically make them think things? You do. It doesn't require a little electric prod thingy, just the right stimuli. All you have to do is direct a particular noise at someone or show them the right kinds of images at the right time, and you activate memes in the same way an invasive probe might make you taste oranges. That's exactly what happens when I write, "Don't think of a black cat."

Those are the first two concepts in memetics. We have a "meme" (a unit of meaning) for ideas floating around in our heads with all their collected associations, and "stimuli," triggers we can send each other to activate memes. We enter each other's minds through the senses. The third concept, meme activation potential, gives far more precision for how we interact with each other.

Meme activation potential, or MAP, is the likelihood that a given stimulus is going to trigger the meme we want it to trigger. If you think about it, every stimulus we throw at each other has some likelihood of activating a meme.

Maybe you and I are at the same dinner table and you're sitting across from me. You have the salt next to you, and I would really love it if you passed me the salt. What can I do? What are some stimuli that I can throw at you so they activate the idea in your head that I want the salt and you could pass it to me? I could mime the saltshaker. You would (hopefully) understand and pass the salt. Maybe I could simply say the word "salt." You would probably understand that means I want the salt.

But let's get ridiculous for a minute. There are other stimuli I can throw at you that are unlikely to make you realize I want the salt. Maybe I stick my tongue out. You look at me blankly.

If the likelihood you'll understand what I'm intending is very, very low, that would be considered low meme activation potential. On the other hand, I could make some sounds that are very likely for you to understand what I mean. For example, I could give you audible stimuli with high meme activation potential. In that scenario, I would say, "Please pass the salt." You're probably going to understand what that means.

But I didn't use words. Not really. We think of primitive humans living in caves grunting at each other, but we are still grunting. If enough of us use the same noise to refer to the same meme, we call that noise a "word." If we use the same collections of noises to refer to the same collections of memes, we call that "language." But there's no such thing as a word. No such thing as a language. Not really. Just stimuli we all share.

We call them words, but when we speak, we just use noises with high meme activation potential. That's all "language" is. That's all a "word" is. What we call "language" is just a collection of stimuli with high meme activation potential. If the stimuli are *audible stimuli* with high MAP, then those are "words" you understand. If the stimuli are *visual stimuli* with high MAP, then that would be writing or sign language. Consider what you are looking at right now as you read. This book is a collection of visual stimuli with high meme activation potential, not "words." There's no such thing as "words." Just visual or audible stimuli with a high likelihood you will understand my meaning.

We know there's a range of low to high MAP. There's also moderate MAP, somewhere in the middle. Let's think of another example. Maybe you're on the beach and you're walking along the sand. You know how sometimes the waves drag rocks and shells with their ebb and flow? Maybe the waves will leave some little scribbles and lines in the sand, but it's just gibberish and nonsense. Those lines are visual stimuli with low meme activation potential. The scribbles on the sand don't really activate any ideas in our heads. Maybe if we walk down the beach, we see curvy seaweed that, if we squint a certain way, looks like actual word scribbles, and we go, "Huh. It kind of looks like the word for 'dog.' Cool." We know no one has actually written the word "dog," but it's visual stimuli with moderate MAP.

As you walk further down the beach, you see someone clearly did write D, O, and G in the sand. Boom. You think dog very, very clearly. There aren't letters written in the sand because, like words, letters don't exist. They are just shapes in the sand somebody made with their finger. They are just visual stimuli, but visual stimuli with high MAP. We now have a range of stimuli: those with low meme activation potential (which don't really mean anything to us, just noise), moderate meme activation potential (which means there's some likelihood we'll get it but it's ambiguous and we're not sure), and high meme activation potential (which means we're absolutely going to get it).

Why is this useful for us in our day-to-day communication? Because it's easy for us to blame other people for failing to understand us. Maybe the problem is that we, as senders, weren't using stimuli with high enough meme activation potential. It's very much our responsibility to try to make sure we're using high meme activation potential as communicators to avoid misunderstandings where possible. Vice versa, if we are the receiver, we can ask ourselves, "Am I receiving enough MAP with these stimuli? What needs more clarification? Can I give myself higher MAP if the other person isn't giving enough MAP, and what might that look like?"

We talked about what a meme is. It's not just a funny picture. It's a unit of meaning, any concept you have in your head with its associations, its likes, dislikes, memories, in one package. We walk around with a bunch of memes in our heads, which, over the course of our lifetimes, come to be associated with different kinds of stimuli. A single stimulus is anything that triggers one of the five senses. Arguably, there are no such thing as words or letters, just stimuli with more or less meme activation potential.

MAP can be really low or it can be really high or somewhere in the middle. Think of MAP as an adjective we use to describe the stimuli we throw at each other when we communicate. MAP is the likelihood any given stimulus will activate the meme we want it to activate.

If you can wrap your head around these three ideas (first, what exactly is a meme; second, how we associate memes with stimuli; and third, how those stimuli have varying degrees of meme activation potential), that will give you a very sharp insight into exactly what it is all of us are doing every day when we interact with people.

10 Tips on Understanding

1. Anticipate and avoid environmental noise

Many social functions take place in loud restaurants, which work against communication. Getting to know someone? A local coffee shop may be better than trivia night at the bar. Similarly, many video calls suffer from unpredictable Wi-Fi, but using an Ethernet cable from the start provides a more reliable signal.

2. Watch for invisible forms of noise

Environmental noise is easy to spot and eliminate; but physical, psychological, and semantic noise often go unnoticed, leading to distractions or misunderstandings.

3. List the times when you tend to experience more psychological noise

Does your mind wander in arguments as you prepare your response? Do you get especially emotional with certain people? Knowing when to be more alert will help you avoid psychological noise more often.

4. Minimize invisible forms of noise

Psychological noise? Bring your mind back to the conversation. Semantic noise? Specify what you mean or ask what the other person means.

5. As a sender, assume responsibility for creating understanding

Many people put the onus on others to understand them, preempting themselves with a phrase like "please don't misunderstand me." As a sender, take responsibility for encoding your message with the best symbols, using the most efficient channels, and avoiding noise.

6. Notice and limit when you use jargon outside of work

Professions in medicine, education, the military, finance, and sales are replete with unique abbreviations, phrases, and titles. Within the profession, this jargon serves to avoid semantic noise. Outside the profession, it serves to alienate and confuse.

7. Solicit questions openly to make sure you are understood

A good way to fill the communication gaps created by noise is to have others ask you questions, but people are often afraid to ask questions for fear of looking dumb. Fielding questions in an open-ended way like "What questions do you have?" or "What can I clarify for you?" presupposes that questions exist and is more likely to work than a closed, yes/no solicitation like "Are there any questions?"

8. Use high MAP for clarity

Clear messages are helpful because they have high MAP. Avoid ambiguity. Be specific. Use vocabulary that's precise.

9. Expect others to use low MAP

The people you're talking to may not have a tacit grasp of MAP or have read a book like this one. Brace yourself for ambiguous speech with low MAP. Lend them your patience

10. To create inside jokes, use stimuli that has high MAP for your friends but low MAP for everyone else

That's all an inside joke is. Stimuli with high MAP for those in-the-know, but low MAP for those who are not. Also, I just lost The Game.

Chapter 2

Avoid Misunderstanding

> "'Most of the trouble in life comes from misunderstanding, I think,' said Anne."
>
> — Lucy Maud Montgomery, Anne of the Island

It would be pretty cool if we could make a robot that could communicate well, but that is exceptionally hard to do. Even our best virtual assistants like Google and Siri have a hard time keeping up with regular human conversation. That's because robots are programmed to do things in a way that makes sense. When they speak, they're speaking with a specific intention, and when they listen, they're listening for specific actions. Humans, on the other hand, speak a little bit weird. We're used to the way we speak because it's all we've ever known, but when you really start to analyze the way people talk, you realize people speak a lot of gibberish to each other. Yet, we manage to find a way to make sense of each other's gibberish.

Gricean Maxims

The philosopher and linguist Paul Grice first started articulating the different ways we speak gibberish to each other and how we can make sense out of it. What Grice gave us are now known as the four Gricean Maxims.[7] These are rules we assume other speakers abide by when we talk to each other. As long as we all constantly adhere to these same four rules, then we're able to make sense of each other's gibberish. What are the four different things that we are assuming all the time?

The first is called the **Maxim of Quality**, which suggests we tend to assume people are giving us true information, or at least information that they believe to be accurate. Now, why is this useful? Because we don't actually give each other literally true information all the time. In fact, we often give each other very inaccurate information, but we're still able to make sense of each other.

Here's an example. Maybe you invite your friend out for a cup of coffee, but your friend says they have "a ton of papers to write." What is your friend actually saying? You and I have gotten used to speaking human gibberish, so we understand our friend is turning down our invitation to go grab a cup of coffee.

But let's take a closer look at what they said about having a ton of papers to write. Come on. No, they don't. A *ton*? That is way too many papers. You can start today and be writing for the rest of your life. What the friend said isn't actually true, but thanks to the maxim of quality and our tendency to assume that people give us true information, we assume they have "a lot" of papers to write and therefore can't grab a coffee.

Even though it's not literally true, if we assume it's accurate, we can calculate they have a lot of papers to write, which takes up their time, so they can't go grab a coffee. Fair enough. That's the maxim of quality. We tend to assume people give us information that's true, even if it's not technically true.

The second Gricean Maxim is the **Maxim of Quantity**, which suggests we tend to assume people are giving us enough information to be understood, not too much information so that it's excessive or too little so that it's not enough.

This is why we are still able to understand each other with very little information. You invite a friend out for lunch, and they shrug and say, "Eh." They really haven't given you very much information at all, but you can tell it's a no. How can you tell? Because you are adhering to the maxim of quantity. You assume your friend has given you enough information to be understood. You infer the person has a lot of things on their plate and won't be able to make it.

Equally, this is why you might understand a talkative friend. If you were to ask if they wanted to grab lunch and they just started rambling on and on, telling you about all the things they have to do, you can tell it's a no. The most efficient response would have just been "no," maybe with a headshake and a sigh. But when your friend lists all their responsibilities, you know the real answer before they start their entire novel's worth of information. That's unusual and unnecessary. If they start doing that, they've flouted the maxim of quantity, and you can still make sense of them by assuming they've given you sufficient information.

Speaking of talkative friends, if you're worried that you might be the overly chatty one, you may benefit from The Traffic Light Rule.[8] Radio host Marty Nemko suggests that for your first 30 seconds speaking, you have a green light. Your listener is engaged and following along. After 30 seconds, your light turns yellow. Your listener is half-listening and is waiting for you to make your point or wrap it up. At 60 seconds? Red light. Stop talking. If they want more, they'll ask follow-up questions.

Of course, this is not a strict rule. But for any of us who have been running red lights without realizing it, this may be a lifesaving way to read the room. Do people's attention seem to wane when you speak? Do you ever wonder why you talk a "normal amount" while other people seem so "quiet"? Do you dominate the conversation as opposed to trading the speaking floor with others in roughly equal amounts? If you answered yes to any of these questions, The Traffic Light Rule might be your new conversation cheat code.

The third Gricean Maxim is the **Maxim of Manner**, which suggests we should be clear when communicating information. If we assume adherence to this maxim all the time, then we can understand each other when we are, on paper, not being clear. For example, if we ask our friend for coffee, and they reply that they have a thing to get to, we assume they have a meeting or some pre-planned social obligation to get to. But what is a "thing" to get to? The word "thing" is so imprecise it's useless. "Thing" could literally refer to anything. They may as well say, "Sorry, I've got a noun to get to." Why do we still understand them?

In Hawai'i, there's a perfect go-to phrase to act as a vague stand-in during conversation. The phrase is "da kine." Where are we going? We gotta go da kine. What are we doing? We gotta pick up da kine. Da kine is a verb. It's a place. It's a person. Everything we need is da kine. The expectation behind da kine is that there is enough shared understanding between sender and receiver that the receiver can quickly piece together what's being referred to without asking. There's an intimacy to the use of da kine that you don't really get from other verbal placeholders like "whatchamacallit."[9] As long as we adhere to the maxim of manner, then da kine is all we need. You gotta go da kine? Okay, see you later.

People speak vaguely. But because we assume people speak clearly *enough* to be understood, we can all still make sense of each other.

The final maxim is called the **Maxim of Relation**, which suggests speakers should give relevant information. We assume people stay on topic, which is why we can make sense of them even when they go off topic, which happens all the time. So much of our interactions with people include people going off topic and not answering questions. But as long as we all assume we're staying on topic, we can make it through.

For example, we ask our friend out for coffee, but they reply it's their sister's birthday. What does someone's birthday have to do with grabbing a cup of coffee? Absolutely nothing at all. We didn't ask our friend if any relatives were having a party or what the theme might be. We didn't even ask what their evening plans were. Instead of an answer to our invitation, we heard about some other irrelevant plan.

It makes as much sense as if they had replied their dog was green. That is as on-topic as it's my sister's birthday. Both are totally off-topic, but we can make sense of one of them. It's harder making sense of the dog being green as an adequate response, but we can make sense of the birthday as an adequate response. Why? It's because we're still adhering to the maxim of relation. We assume that what our friend is telling us is related to our coffee invitation. Having a birthday party suggests they have to be at the party, which means they can't be out having coffee. Now we understand, but it's hard to make that same kind of logical rationale for "my dog's green." It's off-topic, but off-topic in a way you can't relate to the conversation even if you assume your friend is staying on topic.

We spend a lot of time telling each other gibberish, but as long as we assume people are giving us true information, then we can understand them thanks to the maxim of quality.

We often give each other very little information like "eh," sighing, or even texting the letter "K." We give too much information when we ramble on and on. But if we assume people give enough information, then we can understand insufficient or excessive gibberish thanks to the maxim of quantity.

What about clarity? We give each other ambiguous information all the time. We say things that have multiple meanings. If we assume people give us clear enough information, then thanks to the maxim of manner, we understand each other's ambiguities.

Thanks to the maxim of relation, even if people respond with something off-topic, we assume they're staying on topic, and we understand each other.

We speak all kinds of gibberish, but thanks to the four Gricean Maxims that describe the expectations coming from both the speaker and listener, we can still find ways to understand each other in our everyday interpersonal interactions.

Speech Acts

We've talked a lot about communication in abstract terms, but what about everyday life? Let's start with speech acts.

If you've ever seen a movie with Iron Man in it (there's, what, about 70 of them now?), it's easy to be amazed by all the different inventions he's built. He's got blaster gloves and rocket boots and lasers. Let's focus on Jarvis, though. If you're not familiar, Jarvis is the computer Iron Man talks to. Like Siri, only Jarvis is way more powerful.

If you ask Siri to tell a joke, Siri will go and search the Internet for a joke. On the other hand, if Iron Man asks Jarvis for a joke, Jarvis understands sarcasm and cracks jokes of his own. Jarvis *has* a sense of humor. That's why Jarvis is so amazing—he understands human communication. It seems nearly impossible to build a robot to understand human communication, when we ourselves don't understand communication entirely. Truth is, there are many times when we talk to each other, we use statements that don't make sense. For example, if you're wrapping up lunch with a friend, and they ask if you're going to eat your fries, we understand our friend is asking permission to eat our leftover fries. If we tried building our own robot, and we asked if it was going to eat those fries, our robot would not interpret the question as one of intent. If it answers no, and we reach over to eat the fries, the robot will ask why we are eating its fries.

Here's another one. You come home after a long day, and your family member is watching TV on the couch. You're always reminding them to clean up, so it's no surprise to see a jacket in the middle of the floor. You ask, "Whose is this?" We know you know whose jacket it is. We understand you're requesting that your family member pick up after themselves. Imagine if the family member simply said it was theirs and kept watching TV. You would probably not be very happy about that.

You and I somehow understand when we ask questions, we're not always looking for the literal answer. Even though I posed a question with a question mark, my intended meaning wasn't to ask a question at all. Even though I asked about your intentions with your fries, I'm seeking permission to eat your fries. It's not always the case that words' literal meanings are important but rather the *intended* meanings behind those words.

To understand what these different kinds of intentions are, we have to talk about Speech Acts. Developed by philosophers John Austin and John Searle,[10] there are six speech acts to know about. If you understand these acts, you'll be able to see what people around you are *actually* doing every time they interact with you. It will also allow you to be more deliberate with your own language to avoid being misunderstood.

The first act is called the **Assertive Speech Act**. This is about conveying information as it is. It's key to remember that we're not using "assertive" as a synonym for confidence or being self-assured. In this context, it means stating facts. If you're giving somebody driving directions, you're using assertive speech acts.

The second act is called the **Commissive Speech Act**, which is a promise to do something. It is a commitment. Whenever we commit to something with our words, we perform a commissive speech act. If someone in your household mentions it's garbage day, and you reply, "Got it," what does that mean? It means that you have agreed to take out the garbage.

You could say it explicitly ("I will take out the garbage"), but as we've gone over before, our spoken speech is not usually explicit or literal. We frequently talk around our intention. If a robot reminded us about the garbage, and we told the robot, "Got it," the robot might be confused since you aren't literally holding the garbage and it is looking for explicit and literal communication. As non-robots, you and I know it's a commissive speech act promising to take out the garbage.

The third speech act is called the **Directive Speech Act**, where you direct someone to do something. For example, you tell your roommate, "Take out the trash right now."

Sometimes stating information can be a directive. The sentence "Tomorrow's trash day" doesn't seem to literally command anything. Since it's relaying information, it seems like it's just an assertive speech act. But you and I know that's not just a regular assertive speech act. It's actually looking for compliance. We're looking for an action to be taken once we've delivered the sentence. If tomorrow is trash day, then someone needs to take out the garbage.

This comes up frequently in relationships, and it will be very important to understand, otherwise, it will cause lots of friction. If I were to get dressed because my wife is waiting on me, and my wife says to me, "Is *that* what you're wearing?" it's probably not a question. If I took her question exactly at face value and affirm that, yes, this is what I'm wearing, this is what is currently on my body, then I'm clearly missing the point. As you know, my wife's question really means that I should go change. She's really saying I look ridiculous, that I'll embarrass her because I'm wearing hot pink pants and an ill-fitting sherbet orange t-shirt to a funeral. My wife used a directive speech act when she asked her question because she was commanding me to go change. It's important to learn how to identify these acts to avoid problems.

The fourth speech act doesn't often take place in regular conversation, but it's useful to know because it shapes a lot of the things around us. The **Declarative Speech Act** occurs when we use words to change something in the world. That sounds a bit abstract but bear with me for a second. Whenever we use our words to change something in the world, we have now given it a title or its function in some way. A couple of people who love each other very, very much are standing in front of a room full of their friends and family. There's an official-looking person standing in front of them, and that person says that the couple are now husband and wife.

They're married, but they didn't used to be married. They used to be fiancés, but the moment somebody in a position of authority makes the announcement they are married now, they become married. Their status in the world has changed, both in a legal sense and a personal sense by the ceremony and their marriage license. When you got your driver's license, the City and County declared that you were a driver. Your driver's license is a little declarative speech act. You didn't used to be a driver but now you're a driver.

These are some nice examples, but let's go for a sad example. You walk past a couple and overhear one of them say, "It's over." That was a breakup. They used to be a couple, but now they're not. How did that happen? Because one of them used a declarative speech act changing the status of their relationship.

We actually have to declare people dead. We think somebody is dead when they just stop being alive but being dead is hard to define. Rumor has it the phrase "saved by the bell" originated because sometimes people would wake up in their coffins. Old gravekeepers put ropes with a bell on the end so if someone was accidentally buried alive, and they woke up in the middle of the night, they could ring the bell, alerting the gravekeepers (working the "graveyard shift," another common phrase) to dig them back up. This urban legend may or may not be true, but it illustrates how death is not as simple to diagnose as it may appear.

Even a lack of a heartbeat isn't a perfect indicator of someone's "deadness." Doctors look for a heartbeat, and if there is none, they give compressions, use a defibrillator, and any number of medical strategies to bring the heartbeat back. We used to think breathing was a good indicator if someone was dead. But respirators can breathe for people who have lost the ability to use their lungs, they're not necessarily dead even if their lungs don't work. When we bring semantic meaning into the world about the state of "aliveness" or "deadness" of a person, we would declare, or pronounce, the person as dead. A doctor does this by pronouncing time of death.

The next is the **Interrogative Speech Act**. The interrogative speech act seeks information. Sometimes this can be very aggressive, like an interrogation, like in the movies where someone shines a light in somebody's face and demands to know where they were on Friday night.

It doesn't always have to be aggressive. It could be casual, like asking, "Where were you the other day?" It's really easy to tell that's an interrogative because I used a question mark. If I spoke the sentence, my voice would probably go up at the end to signal it's a question rather than a statement. Remember that speech acts don't focus on punctuation or specific words, but how those elements communicate a person's intention. For example, let's say we were all going to meet up at six o'clock somewhere. Let's say that somebody is running late, and they show up at seven. We say to that person, "I thought you were going to be here at six" with a rising inflection toward the end.

Now, what are we actually saying? We want to know where they've been. We want to know why they're late. Even though the sentence ends with a period, which might make it look like an assertive speech act, we are really asking them a question, making the statement an interrogative speech act. If we try to build a robot today, and it showed up late, it might respond to our statement by saying, "That's nice you think that. I also think things. I think all kinds of things" because it didn't recognize the question.

It's going to be useful in real life to be aware of when someone is seeking information, as opposed to just stating things because we don't want to mistake a question for a statement.

I've saved the sixth speech act for last because it has the potential to do the most damage in relationships. If you're aware of it, it can dramatically improve the way that you get along with your friends, your significant other, and your family members. It's called the **Expressive Speech Act**. It's not anything particularly functional, like stating information or giving someone a direction. It's about externalizing emotions.

Not all expressed emotions are bad. We can be overwhelmed with positive emotions. Saying, "I love you guys!" or "This song is my jam!" are examples of positive expressions. But if you exclaim you love a song when you're in the car alone, it doesn't really do anything because it's not telling someone something. Even if somebody is next to you in the car, saying, "This is my jam" doesn't really contribute anything useful to the conversation. It's just an overwhelming feeling of joy for your favorite song.

We may be more familiar with negative expressive speech acts. Those are the speech acts when we're really frustrated or irritated. We're bored or upset, and it's bottled up. And then suddenly, *blah*. We vomit out the emotion to someone in our general vicinity. "I can't believe you did this again. You left your jacket on the floor so many times! You're such a moron, you're so irresponsible!" Now that feels kind of bad. Kind of brings the mood down, doesn't it? It's because expressive speech acts, when they're targeted at somebody like this, don't do anything to help. They just make everybody feel bad. Worse, we don't even feel all that much better ourselves after venting it out like that. We're still left with negative emotions.

Expressive speech acts have the potential to be especially destructive. Sometimes we try to get away with it. Perhaps I get mad at my roommate and call him an idiot for leaving his clothes on the floor so many times. The roommate may be hurt and says that I'm hurting his feelings. I backpedal and say that I was just being honest, as if what I had just done was actually an assertive speech act instead of an expressive speech act.

Am I being helpful or informative when I tell someone they are an idiot? Absolutely not. This is what makes it an expressive speech act instead of an assertive one. Expressive speech acts have the potential to be uniquely hurtful in relationships. So, here's the trick. It's difficult but it has the potential to completely change our relationships with people, especially in times of conflict:

Replace your expressives with assertives.

The next time you're in conflict with somebody and you feel an expressive speech act coming up where you want to call them dumb, irresponsible, or that you're sick of them—hang on to it. Don't use the expressive speech act. Instead, use an assertive speech act, an honest, assertive speech act. *Tell* someone how you feel without *venting* how you feel. It's hard to do, but it makes a huge difference.

In our example with the roommate and the jacket on the floor, it's okay to be frustrated that the jacket isn't in the closet. Telling your roommate, "I saw your jacket was on the floor. I know we've talked about this many times, but when I come home at night, and your jacket is on the floor, I trip over it and it's frustrating." This is now an assertive speech act because you are relaying information regarding the jacket on the floor and why it bothers you.

There is a difference between taking our emotions out on someone and letting someone know how we feel. It's okay to let somebody know how you feel. It might be really important for a roommate to know that their behavior has been frustrating for you. Presumably, if they're your roommate, they don't want to harm you, and would prefer to have a good relationship with someone they're living with for who knows how long. If they have been harming you, it might be helpful for them to know how and why their actions harm you. You can't communicate that if you vomit all that negative emotion and take your frustration out on them. This one tip will prevent so many conflicts. Replace the expressive with the assertive.

Ultimately, when people interact with each other, it's not about the words they're using. It's not about the punctuation. It's about the intention behind those words. What kind of act are they trying to perform? They could just be conveying some information to us. They could be pledging a behavior. They could be giving us some kind of command or direction. They could be changing something in the world that is now one way when it didn't used to be that way. They could be performing an interrogative by seeking information. They could claim to be using an assertive when it's really just an expressive, a bubbling up of emotion, like a celebration or venting about your work nemesis.

If you can spot which of these six intentions are actually behind the words people use, that gives you the ability to see what they're trying to communicate. You can cut through the nonsense and the misunderstandings, and vice versa for yourself. If you know your own intention prior to speaking, you can be far more precise. Many of us, myself included, tend to ramble if we don't have a clear direction or specific intention. If you ask yourself what your intention is, if you use the six speech acts to identify whether you are conveying facts, making a promise, giving a command, changing something, seeking information, or expressing emotion, then you can be far more precise with your words, increasing other people's chances of understanding your intention.

Biases & Fallacies

Biases and fallacies provide many ways for our communication to go wrong. Honestly, we could write an entire book on biases and fallacies, but we're going to talk about a small handful that have a direct impact on confounding our communication with others.

You probably know any kind of prejudiced or slanted thinking is a bias. We might be biased because we have favorite people, favorite sports teams, favorite politicians, or favorite movies. These are examples of biases where slanted thinking is in favor of someone or something. Biases can also slant our thinking against someone or something.

A fallacy is any bad logic that appears like good logic. Good logic is where a conclusion will rationally follow from its premises, but in a fallacy, a conclusion does not follow from its premises. These can crop up in our communication with other people so we end up conveying things that might be misunderstood, or we might be deceiving ourselves or others. It's easy to be fooled, to create and spread misunderstanding. We're going to talk about two biases and five fallacies.

Let's begin with an activity called the Wason selection task.[11] This activity uses a deck of cards where each card has a letter on one side and a number on the other side. We draw the following four cards from the pack:

A, D, 3, and 7.

I now claim *if there is an A on one side of a card, there is a 3 on the other side*. You don't know if this claim is true, but you want to figure out if it is. The challenge is to figure out *which cards, and only which cards, you need to turn over to figure out whether the claim is true or false*.

Think it over for yourself for a few seconds before reading on.

You don't need to flip all four cards (A, D, 3, and 7). You want to come up with the smallest number of cards to flip over. Once you decide which cards you would flip over, you flip them. If you're like me, you probably would have gone for the A card and the 3 card. Most people choose to flip the A and

3, which makes a lot of intuitive sense. That's certainly what I would have chosen. But what are the two cards you should actually flip over? The A and the 7. That's kind of strange, right? That seems very unintuitive. Let's walk through exactly why that is.

The claim says, "If there's an A on one side of a card, there is a 3 on the other side." The claim is *not* "If there is a 3 on one side, there is an A on the other." It's a fine line, but it is a real difference. Let's walk through some of these if it doesn't quite click for us. When I was first learning this, it took some time for the explanation to sink in. Intuitively, we want to flip over the A card because we want to check to see if there's a 3 on the back or not. So, of course, we're going to check the A card. The D card doesn't make any sense. It's just noise. D can have any number on it, and it wouldn't make any difference.

Many of us would instinctively reach for the 3 card, but if we turn it around and there's an A on the back, we haven't learned anything new. Even if there's a Z on the back, we still haven't learned anything new because the claim says, "If there's an A on one side of the card, there's a 3 on the other side." *But if we flip the 7 card and there is an A on the back, we have disproved the claim.*

This is a small example of a natural tendency we all have, which is that we are intuitively very good at looking for evidence to *support* what we have heard, but we don't intuitively look for evidence to *disprove* what we have heard. It's not just important to find evidence to support things, we must also try to disprove them.

This exercise brings us to the first and probably the most important bias we're discussing: **Confirmation Bias**. Confirmation bias is our tendency to look for evidence that confirms our beliefs and to not look for evidence that disconfirms our beliefs. If we find a news story that happens to support our opinions, we feel validated for being right. We remember it. We talk about it with other people. We share it on social media. If we ever come across a news story that disproves our opinion, then we have a never-ending list of reasons not to believe it's true. We dismiss it as a fluke or an exception. We certainly don't share it with our friends on social media.

If you are a Democrat and hear a news story about a Republican politician who had a marital affair, it's easy to take this story as evidence that the political right is morally misguided. But if you hear that a Democratic politician had an affair, it's easy to think that the story is just a personal issue and doesn't represent anything inherently wrong with the political left.

No doubt that as you entered the workforce and encountered more people, you started to see a whole slew of people who are exceptionally smart but very dumb. In his book *Why People Believe Weird Things*, author Michael Shermer suggests that smart people believe weird things because they are good at *justifying* things they came to believe for non-smart reasons.[12] Sci-fi author Robert A. Heinlein put it another way, describing humanity not as rational, but as rationaliz*ing*.[13] Rationalizing is what confirmation bias is all about. Confirmation bias creates a filter once our opinion is formed about something. Evidence supporting our belief makes it through the filter. Evidence disproving the belief gets blocked out by the filter. Social media algorithms function as literal filters, showing us information consistent with our confirmation biases and creating opinion echo chambers. We keep reinforcing the ideas we believe even if the idea wasn't necessarily sound.

Here's a fun example. You've heard the word "lunatic." This word has an interesting etymology. The word comes from "lunar," but "lunar" means moon. What would the moon have to do with someone being crazy? There's a long-standing tradition of believing that the full moon causes craziness. Maybe you've heard stories about how people act during a full moon. There are more injuries, fights, all kinds of stuff. If you talk to professionals in related fields, they will confirm it for you. Police officers will testify there are more arrests, break-ins, and assaults during a full moon. If you talk to medical professionals, like nurses that work in the ER, they'll agree that more people get admitted to the ER during the full moon and there are more babies being born.

But if you talk to a statistician, someone who runs the numbers and analyzes the records, they will tell you there is no evidence supporting these claims.[14] There are *not* more people admitted to the hospital or more babies born under a full moon. There are not more arrests or break-ins. Why would so many professionals, experts in their fields, say otherwise? Well, imagine when you're young, you hear that the full moon causes all kinds of craziness. Later, after you finish police academy training and you're making an arrest during a full moon, the action itself confirms the stories you've heard. "Figures," you think as you slap on the handcuffs, "it's a full moon tonight."

We remember the hits. We forget the misses. In fact, we're often not even keeping track of the misses. If you as a police officer hear that a full moon causes craziness, you're not keeping track of arrests you made when the moon was a waning gibbous or a waxing crescent. We're not keeping track of all of that. We're only keeping track of the stuff that we heard about before, and that's exactly how confirmation bias works.

Our first fallacy is **Post Hoc Reasoning**. Post hoc reasoning is sometimes called a "false cause." This is when we assume a causal relationship simply because two things happened in order. Event A happens. Then event B happens. Now we think that A caused B simply because it happened first. But this is not enough to determine causality. Like they say, correlation is not causation. Just because A happened before B, that doesn't mean A caused B.

Time ordering can be very convincing. Roosters crow early in the morning, and after the rooster crows the sun rises. Post hoc reasoning is believing that the rooster caused the sun to rise simply because you observed the rooster crowing first, then observed the sun rising. Superstitions work this way as well.[15] A basketball player, nervous about their first basketball game, buys new underwear and ends up winning the game. The new underwear caused the win, and now they have a lucky pair of underwear.

This kind of superstitious thinking occurs when we start losing control. You can't control the sun rising, just as you can't control whether or not you win a game. The less control we have over a situation, the more psychological control we tend to reclaim through fallacious thinking.

This is visible in sports that have uneven distributions of control. In the game of baseball, if you are at bat and you miss seven times out of ten, you know what they call you? A Hall of Famer. Batters have very little control over the game and even the very best ones will miss the ball 70% of the time. The pitchers are the ones that have far more control. We can observe more post hoc reasoning with batters as batters will develop little traditions before they swing. A player might come up to bat, tap home plate three times, touch their hat, and then be ready to swing.

The next fallacy we're talking about is thankfully very easy to spot. That fallacy is **False Dichotomy**. A dichotomy is a choice between two things. A false dichotomy is a false choice between two things. This is sometimes nicknamed "the either/or fallacy" or "the black and white fallacy." This is easy to spot when we're talking to somebody (especially if there's an argument). We're trying to figure out what our options are, and the other person reduces a complex issue down to just two options. "Either it's my way or the highway." "Either you're with us or you're against us." There might be other choices, but if someone says it's either A or it's B, that's a red flag because they could be presenting a false dichotomy.

False dichotomies reduce our available options. For example, there could also be options C, D, E, and F, but if we present A or B as the only choices available to us, we are engaging in the fallacy and risk polarizing our viewpoints. In fairness, sometimes in life, there genuinely are real dichotomies. For example, a restaurant offering soup or salad is unlikely hiding another tasty appetizer, such as a green smoothie or mozzarella sticks. However, if your partner says you can either come with them to their fancy party tonight or stay home and sulk, that's a false dichotomy. You could also hang out with your own friends, go with your partner for some of their event and return home before it's over, or even go out on the town on your own. In many contexts, if you're ever given A and B as the only options in a conversation or a debate, it's worth being skeptical about.

The next fallacy is tempting to use for evil, but I implore you to use your knowledge for good. The **Straw Man Fallacy** works when two people are arguing with each other, and one will invent a weak version of their opponent's idea and rebut that weakened idea to make it appear they have won the debate. What they're actually doing is going off topic. I'll give you an example. Maybe you and I are having a heated argument about child safety. You say kids shouldn't play in the street because traffic is dangerous. Employing the straw man fallacy, I say that you want to lock kids up and chain them to the fridge, so they never see the sun. How terrible of you.

But that's not what you said at all! It can look like I'm the winner because I'm the one who's looking out for kids because who in their right minds would advocate chaining up kids to their fridges? Your argument that streets are dangerous because of traffic makes sense, but I made up my own version about locking kids up so I could look like an advocate for kid freedom, thereby winning the exchange. People may feel hesitant to call me out because they don't want to look like they're on the side of locking up kids. Instead of addressing your point about the dangers of playing on the street, I changed the subject when I created my straw man argument. This is called a non-sequitur. A non-sequitur is anytime someone's argument goes off topic.

You see this often in political debates. A candidate running for office may say they think that people should undergo a psychological evaluation prior to being able to purchase a gun. The opposing candidate may say in response that the first candidate actually wants to take away all your guns, even though that's not what first candidate said. They said that they want to create certain checks for acquiring new guns but creating a straw man argument makes an opposing ideology easier to knock down.

This can be tempting to use on purpose, especially if the person with whom you're conversing isn't skilled in debate and argumentation. Hopefully you use this more as a receiver to identify it when it happens rather than attacking other people's arguments as a sender. Use this knowledge so you can spot this fallacy whenever it comes up. To bring the conversation back on topic, you can say something like, "That actually wasn't the point I was trying to make. Here's the point I was really trying to make." This brings the discussion back on topic, and you can move the conversation forward.

The next fallacy is a nasty one called **Ad Hominem**. Ad hominem is Latin for "to the person." The way this fallacy works is by attacking the person instead of their argument. Again, this is another example of going off topic. In politics, they call this mudslinging. In third grade, it's just name-calling. It's easy to employ this fallacy, especially if feelings are running high. Maybe you're with a group of friends and you're trying to decide on what movie you want to watch together. One of your friends suggests a movie choice, and you say, "We're not going to watch that because you're stupid, you make bad choices. Look at your girlfriend."

Harsh. Ultimately, this is an ad hominem attack because instead of attacking the movie choice itself, you go for your so-called friend's choices. The movie is not stupid, you're stupid. As proof of your stupidity, I present your girlfriend instead of pointing out that the movie uses too many tired cliches. By attacking your friend instead of their movie choice, you have effectively changed the topic, making the argument off-topic. That's why this strategy is a logical fallacy. It's a non-sequitur. It does not follow. Beyond the response being a logical fallacy, it is also just really mean. It's not nice.

Next is my personal favorite. This fifth fallacy is the **Argument from Ignorance**. This works by coming to a conclusion via a lack of knowledge. Ignorance, by definition, is not an insulting word even though it's often used in a derogatory context. It just means a lack of knowledge. When we have no idea what caused something, we invent our own explanation. "I have no idea what caused X, therefore it was Y."

Here's something fascinating that was happening all over in the seventies and with a brief revival in the nineties. Some farmers noticed that their crops, especially cornfields, would be flat. Weird. A farmer, wanting to see how bad the damage was, climbed up on the roof and saw that the crops were flattened in giant patterns and designs that one could only see from the top-down. Thus, the phenomenon of crop circles was born.[16] The farmer, having no idea how this could happen, would attribute it to aliens. Now, maybe it *was* aliens, but we can't go from "I don't know" to "It was definitely aliens." We need some evidence that guides us from the lack of knowledge to the conclusion.

I have a personal example of this. I remember when I was a kid, probably around seven or eight years old, we would have dinner on these little fold-out TV tables, and I had a favorite cup. You know how kids have their favorite cups. I had my favorite cup on the table, and then, I dropped a fork. When I came back up from retrieving my fork, I saw my cup go *pfft*. It slid, moving on the table all on its own. I freaked out because I wasn't doing it, and I had no idea what was making it do that, therefore, it must have been a ghost. This happened a couple times per year. Then one day I caught on to what was happening. It turns out that when I reached down, my leg pressed against the leg of the TV table, tilting it to the side. When I popped back up, the table would right itself, and the glass would slide. I had concluded it was ghosts, when, in reality, it was only me.

It turns out crop circles aren't difficult to make. A bunch of teenagers eventually admitted to it publicly. They would go out in the middle of the night with wooden planks and a rope attached to it, crafting a type of swing. They used the wood to flatten the corn as they stomped out the shapes. By then, the phenomenon had grown so much that people didn't even believe the kids that had been creating the crop circles in the first place. That's how powerful the argument from ignorance can be.

The argument from ignorance doesn't occur because we're dumb. In a way, it happens because we're smart. We are meaning-seeking creatures. We like having explanations. Our penchant for meaning-seeking has given us penicillin, solar panels, and cartoons. But if we can't find an explanation, we will often invent one.

Let's end with one more bias. This bias can help make us feel better by helping us through the day and making frustrating times a little bit nicer. This is the **Fundamental Attribution Error**. The fundamental attribution error, or the FAE, is whenever we attribute somebody else's negative behavior to that person's character, but if we do something bad, we attribute our negative behavior to our surroundings. There was something in our environment that made us do that. This is a great one to spot while driving on the road and someone cuts us off. I'm sure we have all kinds of colorful adjectives and nouns for that person. They're a bad driver, an idiot, or some other choice words. But if *we* quickly change lanes, and we realize we cut someone off, we might think they were in our blind spot, that it's a one-off thing, or that we really have to use the bathroom and are in a rush.

With the FAE, we judge others for their *actions*, but we judge ourselves for our *intentions*. This is a nice one to keep in mind because this can really get us through the days where we see a bunch of people doing "mean" things and we're getting disillusioned with the world and the people in it. We think they're just a bunch of mean people doing bad things. The truth is that people tend to be unaware. They're probably more like us than they are a one-dimensional mean-spirited villain because maybe *we* were in *their* blind spot or maybe *they* really had to use the bathroom. People tend to be more absent-minded than mean-spirited, which is nice to remember.

So, there we go. We've got five fallacies and two biases. We started off with confirmation bias, our tendency to remember the hits and forget the misses. The other bias that we talked about was the fundamental attribution error, how we judge others for their actions and ourselves based on our intentions. We talked about five different fallacies. We started off with post hoc reasoning, which falsely reasons that a preceding event caused a following event. The false dichotomy splits a choice into just two options. Thirdly, we looked at the straw man fallacy, which is when we create a fake version of somebody else's argument in order to knock it down. Then we talked about ad hominem, which utilizes attacking the person as opposed to the argument. The final fallacy we discussed was the argument from ignorance, which occurs when we jump to a conclusion from a lack of knowledge. Hopefully, if you can spot these fallacies and biases in yourself, then you can be a bit more deliberate about removing them when interacting with other people. If you can spot them when they're coming from others, then you can have a healthier sense of skepticism and avoid the spreading of misunderstanding.

10 Tips on Avoiding Misunderstanding

1. Speak accurately, sufficiently, clearly, and on-topic

Grice's Maxims of Quality, Quantity, Manner, and Relation help us make sense of conversations when people *don't* say things that are literally true, sufficient, clear, or on-topic. But if we can speak in those ways out of the gate, we are more likely to avoid misunderstandings.

2. Choose your speech acts intentionally

You are using speech acts whether you choose to or not. Be intentional with your speech acts. *Why* are you speaking? To share information? To commit? To direct? To change? To ask? To express? What's your goal with this conversation? What's your goal with this *utterance*?

3. Identify the speech acts of others

The person you're talking to is probably not aware of which specific speech acts they are using. A person who angrily insists they are "just being honest" (i.e., supposedly delivering assertive speech acts) may be riding a stream of consciousness, like a rant, which emerges as expressive speech acts. There may be no point other than venting. Alternatively, a partner who asks, "Is *that* what you're wearing?" is not asking a question. They are likely giving a directive speech act—"*Go change.*"

4. As a speaker, remember The Traffic Light Rule

Radio personality Marty Nemko suggests you have a green light for your first 30 seconds, a yellow light for the next 30 seconds, then a red light at 60 seconds. Continue if you are asked follow-up questions; if not, pass the floor to your conversation partner by asking them a question. This is not a strict rule. It certainly differs across cultures and for different relationships, but remembering it might help us avoid burying our point by rambling or exhausting others.

5. Budget some patience for others when their speech seems aimless

As you notice others' speech acts, you may inevitably tire of being on the receiving end of others' streams of consciousness. You'll nod along, inwardly screaming "What's the point?!" Budget a bit of extra patience for them. Their expressive gushing over the latest TV show may be a bonding opportunity for you even if it's not vital information in a work meeting.

6. Replace your expressives with assertives

Don't vent how you feel. Describe how you feel. This is difficult but life changing. Like Aristotle put it, "Anyone can be angry—that's easy. But to be angry at the right person, to the right degree, for the right reasons, at the right time, and in the right way is very difficult."[17] The right way likely involves minimizing our expressives.

7. Spot fallacies when they're presented to you

Other people will communicate ideas to you that are spurious or ill-reasoned. Guard your patience ahead of time and expect it to happen. When you are presented with fallacious reasoning, don't fall for it.

8. Minimize your own fallacies with others

Just because you've read this book doesn't mean you will be immune to fallacies in the future. It's easy to spot others' faulty logic and congratulate ourselves for being wholly rational. But the "I'm right, you're biased" mindset makes us even more vulnerable to biases and fallacies within ourselves. Try your best to catch biases and fallacies in yourself to avoid spreading misunderstanding with others.

9. Identify topics for which you share the hits, but not the misses

We are more likely to share news stories that confirm our beliefs, but not stories that disprove our beliefs. Identify the emotionally charged topics for which you might remember the hits and forget the misses (e.g., favorite political parties, sports teams, pop culture trends, social issues, etc.). Be skeptical of how you approach these topics. Confirmation bias reinforces our opinions because we are great at spotting patterns, not necessarily spotting truths.

10. Consider others' situations when you get flustered with them

We judge others for their actions, but ourselves for our intentions. The fundamental attribution error is a gentle reminder that the people around us who seem off-putting are a product of their environment—just like we are. Their behavior is likely due more to their surroundings than the built-in traits that our initial irritations will tell us. People tend to be more absent-minded and unaware than malicious and mean-spirited.

Chapter 3

Improve Your Relationships

"Love does not consist of gazing at each other, but in looking outward together in the same direction."

— Antoine de Saint-Exupéry

Perhaps the single most important decision we can make in life is with whom we will spend it. Even if romance isn't your area of interest, you will find that many of the principles for happy romantic relationships apply just as well to friendships or professional connections. If you are interested in managing relationships of various closeness, it pays to examine the closest relationships of all. We're going to talk about relationships chronologically in three phases. First, we'll be looking at how people become attracted to one another. Then, we will talk about the communication patterns involved in maintaining healthy relationships. Finally, we will talk about the communication patterns that tend to lead towards breakup and divorce.

Once, I was asked why end the discussion with breakups and why not finish the conversation on romantic relationships by talking about the end of successful relationships. I think that's an interesting question. You can certainly correct me if I'm wrong, but I think relationships, generally, will end in one of two ways (I think it's a *real* dichotomy). Either the relationship *doesn't* work out and the couple separates, or it *does* work out and...someone dies. Since the process of aging is better described by biology rather than communication science, we will be talking about the break-up scenario which is more attributable to communication.

Attraction

Let's start by talking about the beginnings of a relationship: attraction. There are many different types of attraction. There are a few different things that draw us to people, and some of them aren't very intuitive. The more aware you can be of your unconscious attractions, the more of an advantage you can have in your own relationships. When we think of someone as attractive, what does that usually mean? It probably goes without saying we think of the person as being physically attractive.

Physical

We often think of physical attraction as being biological or hardwired into us. Surely, different physical attributes are more attractive because they are objectively better in a partner, right? For example, think about the archetype of a physically attractive woman. We might imagine an hourglass shape with a large chest, narrow waist, and wider "child-bearing" hips. When we picture the archetype of a physically attractive man, we might imagine a kind of inverted triangle: broad shoulders, full pectoral muscles, and narrowing at the waist. A strong protector of the family. But it turns out that these are modern conceptions of attractiveness that didn't always exist. Even just a couple of generations ago, the beauty standard for women that was considered most attractive was a more heavyset body type, which at the time suggested access to resources and wealth.[18] There are even cultures today that still value very different body types than those seen as attractive in western culture.

This doesn't mean all physical attraction is completely arbitrary. Research suggests that across various cultures, symmetry is a good predictor of physical attraction.[19] That is, the more the left and right sides of a person's body resemble each other, the more they will be perceived as attractive. Researchers speculate this might be a good indicator of overall health. If a person is mostly symmetrical, they're probably going to be relatively free of diseases or parasites—good breeding stock. But what research does find over and over again is that a large proportion of what we perceive to be physically attractive is not constrained by our biology but instead by our culture.[20] We tend to be attracted to arbitrary standards that change from generation to generation or culture to culture.

Why is this useful to know about? Not necessarily because we are trying to attract someone else or because we're trying to understand why we are attracted to them. Probably the most useful reason to be aware of how arbitrary physical attraction can be is to be aware of our own self-perception. That is, we tend to be so bombarded with imagery of physical standards around us which we then try to meet, attain, or strive for in some way and almost always fail to achieve. But you know something? The game is rigged. If you ever get a chance to see the start to finish process of what happens in a modeling photoshoot, it can be astounding to watch. Every photo you see in professional print (and nowadays in a lot of non-professional media as well, like social media) has already gone through a touching up process.

For example, eyes often have extra pupil dilation. Legs are often stretched, elongated to the point they are not even within normal human proportions. Necks are often elongated in this way as well. Skin gets retouched, cheekbones contoured, muscles and jawlines all get added definition. The final product is usually one that doesn't even represent a normal human. You would never know just by looking at the final product because we don't have access to the base picture, the original that wasn't touched up. By observing the entire process from start to finish and being able to compare the original person with the final, touched up image, it's easy to see just how dramatically different the final product is. If you have the time, you should do an internet search for before and after image edits of celebrities to see how much of their proportions are changed.

It's important to be aware of how much manipulated imagery surrounds us. We aren't surrounded by images of attractive people as they actually are but by the retouched images of the people as they are imagined to be to meet arbitrary beauty standards.

Photographers will regularly "spray and pray," taking hundreds or even thousands of shots because, statistically, one or two are bound to turn out well. Most of the photos will be rubbish to average, but no one will ever see those. Digital cameras are no longer restricted by the limited rolls of film. Shoot as much as you like, take the absolute best, lucky photos, and retouch those to make them even better. It's not just pictures though. This happens in movies too.

A good example of this was shared in an interview with Hugh Jackman on *The Late Show* with Stephen Colbert.[21] Jackman was there to promote a movie where he played the superhero Wolverine. In the interview, he describes the process of his fitness routine in the days leading up to shooting a shirtless scene. Now, if you ever get a chance to see a photo of Hugh Jackman as a shirtless Wolverine, he's an impressive specimen. Every vein and muscle pops. What Hugh Jackman described in the interview was a fairly disturbing process. Apparently, the way Hollywood actors get their veins and muscles to pop on screen is through a very calculated, deliberate process of dehydration.

As you might imagine, in the weeks leading up to shooting there is a lot of weightlifting, exercise, and meals featuring only chicken and broccoli. But in the final days before shooting a specific, shirtless scene where the muscles and veins need to pop, the actors will drink huge amounts of water. Then they stop hydrating completely for about a day and a half. They urinate and sweat out all the water they drank, leaving them extremely dehydrated. This pulls the skin tightly around the muscles underneath, giving them sharp definition for a few hours that can be used for shooting. After the shoot, the actors resume drinking water so they don't destroy themselves. Colbert joked, "Three days without water, you die. You go halfway to death and then you go, 'Roll 'em!'" Jackman agreed.

It's not just in photographs, but even in movies the people you see simply do not look like themselves. They manipulate their bodies in particular ways to look a very specific way for a very small, specified amount of time. Just long enough to get the shot and just short enough not to do too much damage to themselves (hopefully). This process, I should remind you, takes place even before the footage even hits the editing room for touch-ups.

If it seems like we're spending a lot of time talking about physical attraction, it's because a lot of this process slips under our noses. We have no idea just how arbitrary and constantly changing our cultural standards of beauty are. We also have no idea the degree of touch-ups and manipulation that go into images featuring pinnacles of so-called attraction that surround us, to the point that actors in live-action movies don't even look like the actors themselves in real life.

Social

Setting aside physical attraction, what would come to mind if I asked you how are we attracted to each other in a way that has nothing to do with our looks? I'll bet a lot of us would mention personality. When we think about being attracted to someone because of their character or their personality, what we are really describing is what researchers call social attraction. Social attraction is when we are drawn to someone simply because we have compatible communication styles. I'm talking about the kinds of people you can talk to for hours and hours, and it feels like minutes. Maybe the two of you have a sense of humor that clicks perfectly with one another. Whenever we describe someone as having a magnetic personality or being the life of the party, we are really describing their social attractiveness.

Social attractiveness can, in fairness, have nothing to do with romantic attraction. It's possible for us to find our BFFs in life just because we have amazingly compatible communication styles. I describe it here because we don't often credit that we can become romantically attracted to someone in ways having nothing to do with their physical appearance. It's entirely possible to become attracted to someone romantically just because of our social interactions with them.

This is becoming especially more visible in the twenty-first century as more and more people form relationships online. Turns out that in online, computer mediated relationships, like what occurs when two people meet in a chat room or on a forum about a mutual hobby, people will end up disclosing personal information at about four times the rate of people who talk face-to-face.[22] We're talking about two people who have never seen each other before, who only know each other by their username or avatar. With no physical interaction whatsoever, it is possible for them to become as close to each other as a couple in real life. Computer-mediated communication has given social attraction entirely new weight in the twenty-first century.

Task

The third type of attraction is one I would have never thought of in a million years. Every once in a while, you'll see an online survey or a magazine poll that asks a thought-provoking question: what is a non-sexual thing that you find attractive in another person? Whenever this question pops up in a magazine column, a Reddit thread, a YouTube video, or a personal blog, there's an interesting trend, especially in the responses of women. While men will come up with all kinds of different answers, like when a woman ties her hair up in a ponytail or reaches high up for something just barely outside of her grasp, there is often a surprising amount of agreement in women's answers. One of the most common non-sexual but attractive things to women in these, admittedly, non-scientific, anecdotal, informal conversations, is seeing a man roll up his sleeves.

They are not referring to a man who is wearing his sleeves already rolled up, but the actual process of seeing a man deliberately roll up his long sleeves. In fact, some women don't even realize this was something they found attractive, but the moment they hear another woman bring it up in conversation, their eyes light up as if they have discovered something for themselves or have been validated in a very important way.

Now, for the women who don't find that attractive or for the guys scratching their heads over this, it seems like a very strange thing to be attracted to. Why would rolling up sleeves have anything to do with attraction? To the women who tend to report finding this attractive, it signifies their man is about to get down to *business*. He is about to do *something*—repair a car radiator, fix the spotty Wi-Fi router, repair a leaky sink, whatever it might be. It doesn't matter what the task is, but this guy is about to step into action, and that's attractive. This is what researchers call task attraction, which is when we become attracted to someone simply because of their skills, talent, intelligence, or proficiency.[23]

None of these attraction types need to be restricted to romantic attraction. For example, you've probably been in a situation at work or school where you had to team up with colleagues on a joint project. Who would we prefer to work with? Probably the person we perceive to be very proficient, intelligent, or highly motivated. In the case of social attraction, sometimes we just like spending time around people with a sense of humor. It doesn't necessarily mean that there's a romantic attraction. In the case of physical attraction, sometimes there are people who just want to be around good-looking people but have no intention of courting any one of them. It's important to know about these platonic forms of attraction because so much of what draws us to other people tends to go unnoticed. This does a disservice to romantic attraction, which is almost always contextualized with physical attraction.

One little extra piece of side information you might find useful to know is that the biggest predictors of attraction are propinquity and self-disclosure. Propinquity is just a fancy word for saying exposure to someone (basically being around them). Working the same hours, being on the same committees, and going to the same gym at the same time are all examples of propinquity. Self-disclosure means telling the other person things about yourself, increasing the intimacy of the knowledge as you get to know them better. The greater our propinquity and self-disclosure, the more likely it is mutual attraction will take place. Now that we've discussed attraction, what about an actual relationship?

Love Styles

People see relationships differently. Love styles are how we generally view relationships. The psychologist John Alan Lee suggests that there are six different love styles.[24]

The first love style is called **Eros**. The person who engages this style loves love. For them, physical intimacy is an integral part of a romantic relationship. Someone with a high measure for Eros sees romance as the cover of a romance novel: two beautiful people clasped in each other's arms. Her dress is sheer, highlighting the curves of her body. His shirt shows just enough of his muscled chest as he holds her close to him. Physical intimacy is a significant part of romantic relationships, not an extra on the side. If this person is in a marriage that has less sex for a time, it would feel like something is wrong with the relationship.

The second love style is called **Ludus**. The ludic love style is a recreational form of romance. People who are high in Ludus are not very interested in finding their one soulmate somewhere around the world. They like the butterflies at the beginning of a relationship, the thrill of the hunt, the chase, the sport of romance, and the art of seduction. They jump around from partner to partner or may have a few partners at the same time. They're more interested in the beginnings of relationships, the dating aspect of relationships, and not necessarily looking for a life partner or someone with whom they can raise a family.

The third love style is called **Storge** (pronounced STORE-gay, as opposed to "storj"). Storge is characterized by open communication and very deep levels of trust, particularly marked by friendship. Those with storgic love styles generally can't just go out and meet somebody at a bar or online. Romantic relationships generally grow out of their current friendships. Romance is generally only on the table once they really know someone well. They must be friends with them for a while. A very storgic quote is the old adage that goes, "Love is friendship set on fire."

The fourth love style is called **Pragma**. This is a very deliberate love style, a very calculated approach to romance. People high in Pragma want to make sure that they're very compatible with their partner. They want to have an idea of what they want to be doing as a career, while considering what their partner wants for their career. If they want to be a parent, then they want to know what their partner's parenting style might be to ensure they're compatible. It's a very deliberate, very calculated type of romance. Imagine Spock in a relationship.

The fifth love style is called **Mania**. This is characterized by emotional intensity that includes really high highs and really low lows. When they fall in love, they fall fast. If there's a breakup, they take it hard. For those with a manic love style, romance is often a roller coaster.

The final love style is called **Agape** (pronounced uh-GAH-pay, as opposed to "uh-GAPE"). This is a very selfless approach to relationships. They can't be happy themselves unless they know their partner is happy. If anyone in the relationship is going to experience any kind of distress or suffering, they would rather experience the distress themselves rather than allow their partner to suffer.

Our love styles can change over the course of our lives, but they persist long enough to have significant influence on our relationships. It's also important to mention that no individual love style is the best or right one. There are no "good" love styles versus "bad" love styles. These are just descriptions. They're not judgments. It's good to have an idea of what our style is as we enter relationships because each of them has their strengths and each of them has their weaknesses. For example, someone may think that a Ludus style encourages cheating in relationships, while another person might be grateful for the freedom a ludic partner offers. They do what they like, you do what you like.

Some consider Agape as the best love style because it puts others first. But "selfless" is a very loaded word. For someone whose style is Agape, they may be very easy to take advantage of. It's easy to get walked all over when your main priority is making sure your partner is cared for as opposed to yourself.

None of these styles are necessarily good. None of them are necessarily bad. By building our relationship vocabulary, it gives us more precision in trying to figure out what's going on in our relationships.

Imagine a relationship between someone who is really high in Ludus and the other is really high in Mania. That's going to be a very tumultuous relationship because Mania believes Ludus is their soulmate. Meanwhile, Ludus thinks Mania is cool and fun to hang out with, but they have other people to see this weekend. That's a recipe for disaster. Nobody did anything wrong, no one was malevolent or malicious, but they had different perspectives on their relationship. By being able to reflect on ourselves, identify our love styles along with our partner's, we will gain extra precision as we navigate our relationships.

Satisfaction & Stability

Of course, once two people start a relationship, that's when the *real* work begins. So many movies end with a kiss, but as you well know, once a couple gets together all their work is ahead of them. What are some ways we can maintain healthy, happy relationships where both people are satisfied in the relationship? How can we create stable relationships where two people are likely to stay together? The weird thing is that happiness and stability don't always go together. Maybe you've seen the aftermath of a relationship where someone got dumped, and they didn't do anything wrong. They're broken up about it. They're trying to reevaluate every moment of that relationship by asking themselves what they could have done better. It's possible to do everything right and still have the relationship fail.

To understand what happens during the lifespan of a relationship, we're going to turn to a body of work called **Social Exchange Theory**.[25] Social Exchange Theory tries to describe how we can keep relationships happy and how we can keep them stable. We do this by analyzing a few different variables.

The first variable we're going to talk about is ***Outcomes***. In relationships, there are benefits and there are costs. The way we determine the outcomes of a relationship is by analyzing the total benefits of the relationship. First, consider all the perks of a relationship like companionship, money, or food. Then we subtract the costs: fighting, losing time, losing money, and so on. You can find the outcome of the relationship by measuring the benefits and costs against each other. Outcomes represent a picture of what you have in a relationship right now. In order to determine whether or not that relationship is going to be satisfied and stable, we take the outcome variable and weigh it against two other variables.

The next variable is what researchers call the **Comparison Level** or **CL**. The CL is essentially what we expect in a relationship. It's what we think we deserve. Here's an example of two relationships.

Which relationship do you think is more satisfied?

Relationship 1: O < CL
Relationship 2: O > CL

In Relationship 1, the outcomes are less than the comparison level. What we think we deserve is less than what we are getting right now. Not very satisfying. In Relationship 2, the outcomes are greater than what we thought we deserved. Maybe we thought we would be getting a three and we're getting an eight. That's a great relationship. So, if the outcomes exceed the comparison level, that's how we can have a satisfied relationship.

This just describes satisfaction but remember that we're interested in stability too. If a relationship is stable, it is unlikely to break up. For stability, we need to look at the **Comparison Level for Alternatives** or **CLalt**. The comparison level for alternatives is what we think we can get elsewhere. Everyone has an idea of what a relationship would be like with a different person. This doesn't mean all people are cheaters with one foot out the door looking for the next best deal. It's just that our brains are good evaluation machines. We have an idea of what a relationship would be like with a different friend, with the cute barista, or with an ex. We also have an idea of what it would be like to be single. Being single counts as an alternative.

In light of this information, we have to weigh the CLalt against the outcomes to determine stability. Is the relationship likely to stay together? We're weighing what we have right now versus what we think we can get elsewhere. For example, imagine we're faced with a few kinds of relationships. In one set of relationships, the outcomes are greater than the comparison level for perceived alternatives. In the other set of relationships, the outcomes are less than the comparison level for alternatives.

So, the question is, which of these two relationships is stable?

Relationship 3: $O > CLalt$
Relationship 4: $O < CLalt$

In Relationship 3, where the outcomes are greater than the perceived alternatives, what we have right now is greater than what we think we could get elsewhere. That's a stable relationship. There's no need to go anywhere because the outcomes are so solid, they exceed any of the other possibilities, including being single. In Relationship 4, what we have right now is less than what we think we could get elsewhere. That is an unstable relationship. The grass looks greener on the other side of the fence. Expect someone to jump the fence.

Interestingly, stability and satisfaction change independently of each other. Both of the relationships above could be satisfied or unsatisfied regardless of their stability. Let's ramp it up and combine everything. Relationships are complex, after all.

What do you see in this relationship? Try to decipher it before reading on.

Relationship 5:
O > CL
O < CLalt

If we have a relationship where the outcomes are greater than the comparison level (where what we have right now is greater than what we think we deserve) that is a satisfied relationship. However, the same outcomes are less than what we think we could get elsewhere, making this *satisfied* relationship *unstable*.

It's sad to see the aftermath of a relationship like this. This is when someone can get dumped, even though they did nothing wrong. It's possible for a perfectly happy relationship to end. It has nothing to do with the happiness, the satisfaction, of the relationship. It's about stability. If the comparison level for alternatives exceeds the outcomes, it's unstable.

How about this relationship? What's going on here?

Relationship 6:
O < CL
O > CLalt

Here in Relationship 6, the outcomes are less than what we think we deserve, but they are still greater than what we can find elsewhere. This is a stable but unsatisfied relationship. You're not happy, but you're not going anywhere. This is exactly what happens in a toxic or abusive relationship. It's possible for someone to be very unhappy and not go anywhere.

This is very difficult to witness from the outside looking in. Sometimes we try to help our friends that are in a relationship like this. We try to tell them, "Look how unhappy you are. You used to smile and laugh all the time and now you're so unhappy. You need to leave that relationship." Well, that's just looking at satisfaction, not stability. The person *knows* they're unhappy, but it's not about happiness: it's about the stability. People that are locked in these relationships don't feel like they have any other alternatives. If they feel like the outcomes of the relationship exceed their alternatives, they're not going anywhere. If we're trying to help here, we need to show them that part of the equation. We must show them their alternatives.

Okay, last one.

Relationship 7:
O > CL
O > CLalt

Here's another possibility: outcomes are greater than the CL and the CLalt. What we have right now is greater than what we deserve and greater than the alternatives. This is a satisfied and stable relationship, what I imagine most of us are looking for. If that's what we want to have, then we need to learn to identify satisfaction and stability independently of each other by weighing the outcomes against the CL and by weighing the outcomes against the CLalt. A relationship can be satisfied or dissatisfied and still be very stable or unstable.

Breakups are a big fear, even for those in good relationships. What do we know about breakups? John and Julie Gottman are the founders of the University of Washington's Love Lab, where they specialize in marriage research.[26] The Gottmans would ask couples if they would be willing to participate in some research. If those couples agreed, they would go into the Gottmans' lab and have their arguments recorded. John and Julie Gottman ended up with hours of footage featuring couples arguing with each other. The Gottmans, along with Kim Buehlman and Lynn Katz, analyzed all the recorded couple arguments in an attempt to distill any useful trends or patterns. What they found might just save your relationship.

After sifting through all the footage, they were able to predict divorce with 93% accuracy.[27] That is phenomenal accuracy in any field, especially in the social sciences. One might imagine there would be hundreds of different variables to catalog, but the Gottmans needed only *four* variables to predict divorce. What's more? You don't need to have a Ph.D. to spot these four things. The Gottmans were able to teach their students how to do this. Their students could also spot divorce with 93% accuracy by looking for these four variables. You can too. Would you like to know what they are?

The Four Horsemen

The four horsemen of relationships are unique patterns of communication that pop up when couples are in conflict. **Defensiveness** is the first of the four horsemen, which is when a partner prioritizes self-preservation over conflict resolution. In other words, the person is not willing to compromise, admit wrongdoing, or acknowledge their own mistakes. They are just looking out for themselves, looking out for number one.

Withdrawal is the second horseman, also called Stonewalling. This occurs when one of the partners recedes from the conflict. They are no longer invested in the relationship. They may tell their partner that they don't care, do whatever you want, and so on. The person doesn't want to have any conflict of any kind. They would rather retreat into their shell.

The third horseman is **Criticism**. As an aside, it's important to note that there is such a thing as constructive criticism. It's helpful to point out things we can improve on with each other. This is not what the Gottmans were talking about. This type of criticism entails attacking the partner. "I can't believe you did that again, you're so irresponsible, so dumb." This is the type of criticism that the Gottmans identified. It's not productive or helpful, all that happened was that the person was just venting at their partner, taking frustrations out on them—attacking them.

Now, in newspaper interviews and journal articles, the Gottmans were asked which of the four horsemen was the worst one, and they admitted none of them were the worst. They were all equally bad. However, there was one that spooked them the most personally, which is **Contempt**, the last of the four horsemen. Contempt is a sense of generalized moral superiority to the partner. It means looking down on them, disdaining them.

If you can spot these four horsemen, you can predict divorce with 93% accuracy. There's both good and bad news regarding the four horsemen. The bad news is it only takes one to destroy a relationship. If you're looking at your relationship and realize you only have two of the four, so you're safe, that's incorrect. It only takes one horseman to break a relationship.

The good news is that all four of these horsemen can be repaired. None of these things signal the relationship as a guaranteed failure. It just tells you this is the thing to focus on improving. If you keep having a recurring fight about who's doing the dishes, that's fine. You can always solve who's going to do the dishes. But if criticism keeps coming up in your fight about the dishes, then that signals dishes are not actually the problem. Criticism is the problem there.

Here's something that's easy to think at a distance but is hard to remember in the moment: *often, the way we disagree* is *far more important than what we disagree about*. If these four horsemen start to sneak their way into our habits when we talk to each other, then that is what we should focus on fixing.

Research into happy marriages also revealed a simple number that you might find helpful in combatting the four horsemen.

5:1

A ratio of five to one. That is, it takes roughly five positive interactions to cancel out one negative interaction. We might think one good deed makes up for one bad deed, but negative actions weigh more heavily on us than positive actions lift us. This ratio is what allows us to break even, so if you're looking for an overall enjoyable relationship you will likely need to aim for something more like a 10:1 or a 20:1 ratio.

This ratio is one helpful trick in combatting the horsemen, but you also have another tool at your disposal already. Remember the six speech acts? These four horsemen can only emerge through our expressive speech acts. So, if you've gotten into the habit of replacing your expressives with assertives (like we talked about in Chapter 1), then the horsemen won't be able to get a foothold. How nice!

10 Tips on Relationships

1. Don't get too worked up about others' or your own looks

Most physical attraction standards are made-up generational fads, and a dizzying proportion of what you see showing "attractive" people has been altered. You be you.

2. Build intimacy with time and disclosure

Want to get closer to someone? Be around them more and share with each other more about yourselves. It sounds obvious written so plainly, but propinquity and self-disclosure are powerful bonding ingredients worth remembering.

3. Try to anticipate how your Love Styles will shape your relationship

A relationship with one person high in Ludus and the other high in Mania is likely a ticking time bomb. Two people high in Storge might have an easier time.

4. Minimize costs, maximize benefits

Be aware of your relationship's "outcomes." More shared happy experiences, less bad experiences. This ratio of good to bad will determine your satisfaction and stability. If nothing else, use a 5:1 ratio of positive to negative interactions to break even (it should ideally be higher).

5. To stay satisfied, keep that cost-benefit ratio stronger than expectations

A strong ratio will need to stay higher than your relationship's Comparison Level. Additionally, talk about your Comparison Levels. The more each partner knows what the other wants, the easier it will be to deliver.

6. To stay stable, keep that cost-benefit ratio stronger than alternatives

That outcome ratio will also need to be better than what either of you could get outside the relationship. Keep the grass green on your side of the fence.

7. Help others who are stuck by expanding their perceived alternatives

Sometimes we try to help people in destructive relationships by talking about their happiness. Instead, raise that person's

Comparison Level for Alternatives. That is, give them a way out.

8. Avoid The Four Horsemen

Withdrawal, Defensiveness, Criticism, and Contempt. Don't let them become habits in your conflicts.

9. Focus repairs on The Four Horsemen

Any one of the four can break a relationship, but they can be fixed once you know what to look for. What we argue about is often less important than how we argue about it.

10. Don't take jabs

Don't vent at your partner about your partner. Replace expressives with assertives. You can describe how you feel without taking out how you feel. Difficult at first, but well worth it.

Chapter 4

Learn the Truth About Lie-Detection

"Oh, what a tangled web we weave, when first we practice to deceive!"

— Walter Scott, *Marmion*

Ready for some terrible parenting advice? Tell your young child that you can always tell when they lie because a little dot appears on their forehead whenever they bend the truth. Now, whenever they cover their forehead as they talk, you will know they're lying! Okay, that advice is even more awful than it is amusing. But we do wonder about how to spot lies in everyday life. Much of human communication includes deception from scams, to exaggerating stories, to saving face, to being polite. This chapter focuses on all the ways we deceive each other and how we might catch deception, if at all possible.

So, what do you need to know about spotting lies? We're going to start by examining what kinds of things people do when they're being deceptive. Then we're going to look at different kinds of strategies people have used to try to catch deception. But what do we mean in the first place when we're talking about deception? The British researcher Aldert Vrij came up with what I think is the best definition of deception:

> "Deception is any successful or unsuccessful deliberate attempt, without forewarning, to create in another a belief which the communicator considers to be untrue."[28]

Essentially, the communicator is trying to deliberately make somebody else believe something they don't believe. If I'm trying to give you directions to the grocery store, but I give you wrong directions, then I did not lie. I was just wrong. There was not a willful attempt to mislead you there. On the other hand, if I know that the grocery store is down the road to the left, but I tell you it's to the right, then I was deceptive. Even if you don't believe me, I don't have to successfully deceive you for my message to be deceptive. If a person is willfully trying to create a false belief, that is deception.

You probably don't lie very often in ways that are exploitative or might be called immoral. But you probably do attempt "to create in another a belief which" you consider "to be untrue." That is, you probably deceive. A lot. For example, when someone asks, "How's it going?" which response are you more likely to deliver?

1. *Good, thanks. How 'bout you?* or

2. *Man, my alarm didn't go off again. I don't know what's wrong with that thing. Then as soon as I got out of bed I stubbed my toe, stupid new nightstand—I don't know why we got it, there wasn't even anything wrong with the last one. Did we buy it just because it was on sale? Oh, and that headache is back. It's not too painful, but it's just always there, y'know? I think it's the weather.*

If you went around delivering responses like #2 to every person you saw, you would never get through the day. We often think of deception as a kind of seedy, immoral act. While it certainly can be, it also functions throughout the day as a kind of social lubricant. If we want to catch deception, we need to understand exactly how it works in real life.

Information Manipulation

So how do we deceive? I'm going to introduce you to a body of work called **Information Manipulation Theory**, which tries to describe all the different ways that people construct deceptive messages. To illustrate how we can start thinking about different forms of deception, imagine a little thought experiment that we will call "The Tutu Box." Imagine that every year for Christmas, Grandma gives you the best presents. It's always something hard to get or something you've always wanted. She's gotten you a pony, a PlayStation, the respect of your peers—whatever. Grandma's been hitting it out of the park every single year.

This Christmas, you run into the room, and you see a big golden-wrapped box with a big bow on it, and you know that's Tutu's signature wrapping. You tear the paper off, flip the lid open on the box, and there is...the ugliest pair of socks you've ever seen. Just terrible looking Christmas-y socks, so you can't even wear them any other time of the year. They have reindeers with big antlers sticking out the sides so you can't even hide them by wearing shoes. They're not even Christmas colors. They're orange and purple. They're just ridiculous, ugly socks. In that moment of dread and disgust, as you look away from the socks, you look up and see Grandma's big, innocent eyes staring back at you and she asks, "What do you think of the socks?"

Let's assume two things. First, we do *not* like the socks. Now, there is an off-chance that you are in the .01% of readers who want nothing more than gaudy, gag-inducing purple and orange reindeer socks. If that's you, just imagine a different pair of socks that are genuinely awful to you. Second, we want Grandma to think we *do* like the socks. That's right, we are about to (successfully or unsuccessfully) attempt to create in another a belief which we consider to be untrue. We are about to *deceive*. What are some things that we could say to Grandma? We could say something like "Thanks" and leave it at that. We could say, "Wow, thanks, Grandma. These are...*interesting*." We could get away with that. Maybe we could even say something like, "Wow, thank you, Grandma.

You know, my feet have been *so cold* lately," and that'll put a smile on Grandma's face.

Chances are we don't exactly feel comfortable looking into Grandma's big, innocent eyes, and saying something like, "I *love* the socks, this is the *best present ever.*" This would feel like we're just flat out lying to her face, and it doesn't feel great. This is the first way that people deceive according to Information Manipulation Theory.[29] This is what researchers call **Falsification**, which is whenever we replace true information with false information. We don't like to falsify information; it feels like a moral trespass. A bald-faced lie feels icky. We don't like falsifying even though we do deceive all the time. We create beliefs in others we don't personally believe to be true all the time, and we do it intentionally. So, we tend toward these three other types of deception.

Another way that we deceive is by **Omission**, which is when we leave out really important information. In the Christmas example, we leave out the part where we don't actually like the socks. Grandma looks us in the eye and says, "What do you think of the socks?" We respond, "Wow, Grandma, thanks," leaving out our honest opinion. Deception by omission is sometimes called telling a half-truth. We leave out the vital information we think the other person wants to know.

The third form of deception is **Equivocation**. To be equivocal is to be vague. This is deception through ambiguity, deception by being vague. We can use words with multiple meanings so that we are conveniently misunderstood. For example, if we told Grandma the socks were "interesting," what does interesting actually mean? To you, it can be interesting how stupid the present is. To Grandma, interesting can mean you like the socks. You didn't *lie*, Grandma just *misunderstood*. Right? If your bratty cousin comes running over to you later and accuses you of lying to Grandma, you can remind them you said that the socks were "interesting," which is true (it's interesting how *dumb* they are).

The fourth form of deception is **Misdirection**. This happens when we change the subject, but it doesn't seem like we've changed the subject. Grandma looks us in the eye, "What do you think of the socks?" We say, "Thanks, Grandma! My feet have been so cold lately!" Hold on. That's not what Grandma asked about—she asked for your opinion about the socks. But you didn't give her your opinion, you changed the subject to start talking about your feet. It sounds like you're on topic because it sounds like you enjoy the socks. After all, it solves the problem of cold feet. But we know mentioning cold feet allowed Grandma to think we liked the socks.

Using these tactics, we can purposefully create a belief in someone else that we do not hold. We use falsification by replacing true information with false information, but we usually don't like doing that. It feels immoral and icky. We can use omission by leaving out the important information, use equivocation by being ambiguous, or misdirect by secretly changing the subject on the person.

Falsification: "I love the socks!"
Omission: "Thanks!"
Equivocation: "These socks are *interesting!*"
Misdirection: "My feet have been so cold lately!"

Laid out plainly like this, do you notice anything strange about these methods? Only one of them actually uses any false information. With three out of four of these messages, we could raise our right hand and swear that we told the truth. Omission, equivocation, and misdirection are all true messages. This reveals the big plot twist in deception: *most deception is the strategic use of the truth.*

That's right. When we deceive each other, we don't usually "lie" (replace true information with false information), we tell the *truth*. We just tell a limited version, a fuzzy version, or an off-topic version of the truth. This is partly why deception is so hard to detect. Deception detection is really an attempt to detect...the truth...hidden in and amongst...the truth. That's not like trying to find a needle in a haystack, it's like trying to find one specific hay in a haystack. So, is there any hope? Should we just give up trying to detect deception? Not so fast. There's another body of research that may be able to help.

Deception Detection

If we're going to try to detect deception, there's some good news and there's some bad news. The research contains mostly bad news with a little glimmer of hope at the very end. So, let's start with the bad news.

I'm going to give you a list of cues related to deception that people have used in trainings, seminars, self-help books, and in workshops. You have probably heard that if you learn to spot the right "tell," as they call it in poker, then you can spot a liar. This begs the question, what tells do we look for? Pinocchio had his growing nose, but what about other people? It might be a facial expression or a nervous tick. The Holy Grail of deception detection is to find the tell (or tells) that we can train you to spot in a liar. What can you look for in your coworkers? Your kids? Your spouse? Here is a collection of some of the most common "tells" that have been used by police, investigators, interrogators, and researchers.[30] They have appeared in books, TV shows, and movies. As you look them over, I have a question for you. Which of the following "tells" do you think are NOT useful in spotting deception?

- Decreased eye contact (Maybe liars look at you less as they get nervous?)

- Increased eye contact (Maybe liars overcompensate with too much eye contact?)

- Hand fidgeting (Maybe liars fiddle with their hands?)

- Leg movements (Maybe liars bounce their legs under the table?)

- Sweating

- Stuttering

- Increased blinking (Maybe liars blink more as they get nervous?)

- Decreased blinking (Maybe liars overcompensate and blink less?)

Which ones do you think are useless? Make your guesses because I'm going to reveal the answer in a moment.

A comprehensive excavation for the Holy Grail of deception detection, the real Pinocchio's Nose, was published by Bella DePaulo and her colleagues in the journal *Psychological Bulletin*. They examined the statistical results of decades of research. Over 1,300 estimates of lie-detection that covered 158 of the most popular tells. The list you just read was a small selection of the these tells. So, which ones do you think are useless?

If you voted for any of them, you're correct. The answer is none of them are useful. None of these tells can be reliably used to catch deception. If you train a person to spot any of these, they're not going to be better than anyone else at spotting liars. While DePaulo and her colleagues found some very weak correlations between certain tells and lies, they also had to admit that those tells were "indicative of other states and processes as well." What does that mean?

Imagine you are being questioned by the police for a crime you didn't commit. Is there a chance you might be nervous? Of course! It's not every day you might end up behind bars. Even if you had a cool, stoic exterior, you would almost certainly be more nervous than if you were minding your own business grocery shopping. So, you might sweat or blink more than usual. No doubt the actual criminal while being interrogated would be nervous too. Some people simply do not make eye contact in everyday life. To match societal expectations, some of them might try overcompensating with too much eye contact. The point is: truth-tellers and liars will *both* show signs of nervousness. Truth-tellers and liars will *both* give off tells.

Not only do truth-tellers and liars both give off identical cues, but there are also so many different kinds of lies to try to catch! Telling a made-up story to the cops is clearly lying and it might cause nervous sweating. But what tells do you look for when someone gives a polite "white lie" to protect Grandma's feelings? What about tells for when a couple is angry because they had a fight but put on a smile when they arrive at a party? Who's to say that a tell that works to uncover a crime in the interrogation room would be the same tell for a couple covering up a recent tiff while attending a party? Truth-tellers give the same tells as liars, but even if they didn't, there is a huge array of different kinds of deception in different contexts. There are too many confounds for tells to be useful. Catching liars by watching for tells is like trying to figure out the temperature by watching a thermometer that responds to heat, pressure, humidity, and your mood.

Tim Levine and his colleagues at Michigan State University took some of the most promising cues from Bella DePaulo's excavation that showed at least a slight statistical link with lying, what they called "correlated cues," and tried one more test.[31] They trained a group of study participants to look for these best, correlated cues. They took a second group of people and trained them in nothing whatsoever. They trained a third group in made up, bogus cues. All three groups of people then watched videotapes of people who were either lying or telling the truth and had to guess whether the people were being honest or deceitful. All three groups performed about the same. In fact, there were a couple of instances when the bogus group outperformed the correlated cues group. So, it turns out, when we train people with the best tells, they still don't do any better than chance.

That being said, there is an interesting phenomenon to be aware of. When you train people in spotting deception cues, it can *appear* they get better at detecting deception. In reality, they don't actually get any better at detecting deception, but it can seem as though they do. Let me give you an example. Let's say I'm going to show you videotapes of ten people. It's your job to determine who the liars and the truth-tellers are. Now, on my end, I know I'm showing you five truthful people and five deceptive people, but you don't know what the ratio is going to be like. All you know is that you are going to watch ten people and must detect truth from lies. Imagine I show you all these videotapes. Then you say every single one of them is a liar.

If your response is that all ten of the people lied, then technically your accuracy at catching liars is 100%. You caught every liar. But what was your accuracy for catching truth-tellers? Your accuracy is 0%. In a nutshell, this is what happens when we train people to spot any cue like fidgety hands, twitchy eyes, or stuttering. What happens is that the *lie bias* of these individuals increases, which is just a fancy way of saying they call more people liars. As a result, they do catch more liars, but only because they think more people are lying. It's not because they're accurate at perceiving lies from truth. It's because they're just casting a really wide net with which they're bound to catch liars, but they won't be any good at catching truth-tellers, which is just as important. That's what happens when we train people. It's what happens in the

Secret Service, in police departments, in college classrooms, and psychology courses.

However, there is a light at the end of the tunnel. Our detection skills are better than just 50/50 guessing. It turns out that overall, amongst experts, amongst amateurs with no training, we are all about 55% accurate at catching deception.[32] That's interesting. That is a little bit better than chance because if it were due to chance, purely a flip of the coin, our accuracy would be 50%. But we are reliably above average. So why is that? Because if we can identify where that extra 5% comes from, then maybe we can find a way to expand it. Our ability to correctly identify deception can become progressively more accurate over time.

This is what researchers have been interested in most recently. Again, Tim Levine out of Michigan State gives this interesting thought experiment.[33] Suppose you're taking an exam of 100 true or false questions on a topic you've never studied before. You have no idea what the answers are. What's your overall score at the end? Assuming you have no knowledge on the subject, probably about 50% correct. Your answers are like a flip of the coin every single time. Let's change the scenario slightly. What if only 90 of the true or false questions are on topics you're unfamiliar with? The last 10 are going to be absolute "gimmies." You are going to get them correct no matter what. Some of the "gimmie" questions might be: True or false: you're alive. True or false: you're taking an exam. Ten of them, you're going to nail no matter what. Ninety questions are going to be due to chance, a flip of the coin. With those ten "gimmies," our overall score is now about 55% correct.

This is what Levine says is happening in nature, that trying to detect whether someone is being honest or deceitful is like a flip of the coin. We have no skills of perception, but around one person in ten is a *transparent liar*. No matter what, we can tell if they are being honest or telling a lie. They cannot lie for beans. They will never get away with it. No matter what, whether you're an FBI investigator, whether you're a college student with no training, you can just look at this person and know if they're being honest or deceitful. Chances are, you can probably think of somebody in your group of friends or family who is the transparent liar. Maybe it's you?

There are two approaches that get the most attention and the most research funding. On the one hand, we look for Pinocchio's nose, training observers to spot subtle cues, like the twitching of the hands or stuttering in the voice. But we know that doesn't work. There is no Pinocchio's nose that gives away deception. However, the second method is far more promising. Stop focusing on observers trying to catch lies and start focusing on the deceivers themselves. If we know that one person out of ten is a transparent liar, the real question is how do we increase transparency so that more people start giving themselves away? That's the future of deception research.

If we can create transparency, then it means you don't have to be trained in detecting tells. Anyone could just spot liars if we induce transparency. One way to do that is by requesting people to tell their story backwards. This is difficult for truthtellers too, but more so for liars. This is the new hotness in research right now. If you have an idea for how to induce transparency, then there is a master's thesis or a Ph.D. dissertation in that idea because that's where the research funding is going. Deception research is focused on learning how to induce transparency.

So, this is the very short version. Most deception is strategic truth-telling. Only one of the four types of deception, falsification, involves providing false information. Omission, equivocation, and misdirection are all strategic uses of the truth. When it comes to deception detection, unfortunately, training observers just doesn't seem to do the trick. Doesn't matter what we teach them, the only thing that training does is make people more suspicious. They might catch liars, but it's not because they're accurate. Such training only increases their lie bias and inclination to call more people liars. Research is now focused on learning how to induce transparency to help us spot liars.

10 Tips on Deception

1. Be forgiving if you detect someone using deception as social lubricant

A person may be equivocating to spare themselves or you the embarrassment of their own oversharing. Deception often gets a bad rap (and rightly so when it's used to exploit others), but as a social lubricant, it is a natural part of communication.

2. That said, stay as truthful as you can

Don't take that last tip as carte blanche to go on a lying spree or excuse all others' exploitations. Deception might help some basic social functions from time to time, but we should still do right by each other.

3. Ask yourself, "Can I verify this elsewhere?"

Spotting falsification is difficult. False information can seem just as true as honest information. If we can corroborate the story from other sources, we can more reliably believe it.

4. Ask yourself, "Is this enough information?"

Someone attempting to deceive you by omission will leave out details you would find relevant. If you don't feel you have a complete picture, ask follow-up questions.

5. Ask yourself, "Could this be interpreted in multiple ways?"

Equivocation relies on being misinterpreted. If what you've been told could be interpreted in multiple ways, ask for clarification. "I don't want to misunderstand you, what do you mean by…"

6. Ask yourself, "Is this on-topic?"

If someone deceives by misdirection, they will subtly change the subject. Bring the topic back. "How's the progress on your presentation?" "Oh good, you know we have such a great team." "You really do! Have you been able to create the slideshow yet?"

7. Stop looking for Pinocchio's Nose

The "Holy Grail of deception detection" is a tell, or list of tells, we can train you to spot in others to catch their lies. It probably doesn't exist. Decades of research suggest catching lies is more about sender transparency than observer perceptiveness.

8. Be skeptical of lie detection tricks

Research finds that training people to spot lies does not help, but that's not a very fashionable message (it's not very memetic). Television shows, movies, even books, seminars, and workshops often tout lie detection tricks. Receive them with a very large grain of salt.

9. Avoid developing a Lie Bias

The more you learn about lie detection tricks, the more people you think are liars. This does not make you more accurate (or fun at parties).

10. If you're going to attempt detection, find the transparent liars

Talking to the right *people* is better than spotting the right *tells*.

Chapter 5

Read People

"People may not remember what you said, but they will remember how you made them feel."

— Maya Angelou

Every single time we communicate, we're communicating two messages. First, is the actual content of the message, like "Go grab the mail" or "What time is it?" The second message we are communicating is a *relational* message. We're always giving commentary on the nature of the relationship. Is the relationship one that's cooperative? Is it one that's hierarchical and competitive? Is it hostile? Is it condescending? Is it supportive? Is it fond? Your relational message is largely shaped by your nonverbal cues.

This chapter has the potential to mess up your interactions with people because you can start over-analyzing everything, at least for a little while. But you will also notice more of what's happening around you. You will, like Sherlock Holmes describes, not just see but observe.[34] We're going to talk about body language and reading people and all kinds of fun stuff spread over several different categories so the content is more bite-sized.

Nonverbal communication is any communication without words. A high five, a thumbs up, a shaka, an "ok" sign, an angry face, or a smile are all forms of nonverbal communication, but you probably knew that. A more obscure example might be clearing your throat (*ahem*) to signal you want to say something during a rousing conversation amongst friends.

What do you think Morse code is, verbal or nonverbal? You could communicate a message to someone across the room by blinking your eyes, by tapping on the wall, by flashing lights from a boat, but it's *verbal* because Morse code is being used to spell out words. Even though no one is speaking, Morse code still uses words. Sign language would also fall into this category. Sign language is a language. It is verbal communication because it uses words. It has its own vocabulary, grammar, and different dialects. If our communication uses words, then it is considered verbal communication whether or not we are using our voices. If our communication doesn't use words, it is considered nonverbal.

Harkening back to Chapter 1, you might say that verbal communication involves stimuli with high meme activation potential. Nonverbal communication is stimuli with low meme activation potential.

There are many ways to communicate nonverbally. There are two main categories: body codes and contextual codes. Body codes require the use of your body, while contextual codes require additional types of contexts to be understood.

The four body codes are **kinesics**, **oculesics**, **proxemics**, and **haptics**. There are some familiar-looking words in there. Kinesics might look like it has something to do with kinetic energy, while oculesics contains the same root that forms "ocular." Proxemics is similar to proximity, and haptics might be more familiar to gamers who need to change the haptic controls on their device.

Kinesics

Let's start with Kinesics. Kinesics and kinetic both come from the same Greek root *kinēsis*. Kinesics refers to non-verbal communication through movement. Most people are inherently aware of kinesics, even if they don't actually call it kinesics. For example, forms of nonverbal communication such as body language, hand gestures, and facial expressions are all forms of kinesics.

While certain facial expressions are culturally specific, research suggests that a number of facial expressions are universal and can be found across cultures. One of the most well-known researchers in this field is Paul Ekman, a psychologist interested in how facial expressions manifest across cultures. Ekman and his colleagues' research, published in in the 1970s and 1980s, indicated that some emotions appear to hold cross-culturally.[35] People smile using the same muscles across cultures, whether they're in the mountains of Papua New Guinea or the local guy down at your corner store. Even people who have never seen a smile, such as those who have been blind from birth, smile using the same muscles as sighted people. Our smiles are not learned. They are innate.

Fun fact: you can tell the difference between a real and fake smile. A real smile reaches the eyes. A smile is composed of two main components, a voluntary one and an involuntary one. The voluntary component uses the *zygomatic major* muscles near your cheeks which pull the ends of your mouth upward. The involuntary movement uses *orbicularis oculi* muscles encircling our eyes which activate when we're genuinely happy. This movement is also what causes crows' feet, but those type of wrinkles only mean you smile genuinely frequently; my mom calls them smile lines. These lines form even when the muscles are at rest due to a loss of collagen and elasticity in the skin. A smile is considered "fake" when only the voluntary zygomatic major muscles are active, without the movement in the orbicularis oculi muscle.

Genuine smiles are referred to as Duchenne smiles due to the activation of Duchenne markers. Duchenne markers are named after Guillaume-Benjamin-Amand Duchenne, a French neurologist (and first-name hyphen collector), who investigated human facial expressions in the 19th century. Duchenne used questionable methods that would raise a lot of eyebrows today, sending electric currents through research participants to modify their facial expressions. Duchenne identified two types of smiles: the one we call a "fake" smile, where only the zygomatic major muscle is involved, and the "real" smile, where the orbicularis oculi muscles are also involved.

Facial expressions, like the ones Duchenne investigated in his experiments, are one form of kinesics. Another form of kinesics are hand gestures. There are many kinds of hand gestures. For our purposes as communication crafters, we can consider two categories of gestures. The first group is known as **adapters,** which consists of any gestures that are self-comforting. For example, if someone gives a speech, they may wring their hands, twirl their hair, or tap their fingers to self-comfort their nervousness.

Another group of gestures, called **illustrators**, are more deliberate, metaphorical gestures that stand-in for our ideas. For example, if someone says, "I caught a fish and it was this big," while holding their hands out with a space between their palms, they are using this gesture to illustrate the size of the fish. Another example might be if a person says, "There are three steps to reeling in a big catch," while holding up three fingers.

In addition to facial expressions and hand gestures, we can also examine gait. **Gait** refers to the way we walk, which conveys a lot of nonverbal information about ourselves.[3][6] For example, in one study from the *American Journal of Human Biology*, researchers conducted an experiment to see whether men were considered more attractive based on their movements, specifically, the way they walked. They found male strength was interpreted through movements or, for the purposes of our discussion, *gait*.

The last item in kinesics is **interactional synchrony**, which refers to people's kinesic behaviors as they start to get along with each other. When people hit it off and get along, their interactions begin to synchronize, that is, they behave like each other. This is cool to watch. If two people are in a meeting or hanging out, and one person gets interested, gets higher energy, and leans forward, the other begins to mirror this behavior. The other person gets higher energy and leans forward. If one person relaxes, takes a deep breath, and leans back, the other follows suit. The other person relaxes and leans back. Sometimes this is given the nickname "mirroring." Some say mirroring is a good strategy to use in a job interview because if you mirror the interviewer, you can gain rapport with them and have a good interview.

I'm a little cautious to give this advice myself for a couple of reasons. First, mirroring is very common knowledge, and it's likely interviewers can spot the tactic. Secondly, if you get caught, that sucks. If you try to mirror on purpose, it's usually not mirroring but mimicry, which ends up looking plastic and artificial. That said, learning about interactional synchrony is still useful, but it may not be the best way to create rapport. Rather, use it as a rapport thermometer.

If you're in an interview, and you're wondering how it's going, be self-aware for a second. Take a look at the nonverbal behaviors performed by you and your interviewers. If you are acting like each other, it's probably going pretty well. This can be a lot of fun to deliberately try out with a group of friends too. You may realize you and a friend are starting to mirror each other. If so, see if you can start to guide their actions by changing your own. Lean in. If they lean in...you got 'em! Interactional synchrony can be fun to play around with.

Fun fact about kinesics—couples who have been married to each other for a very long time start to look like each other over the decades. That's pretty weird—why would that happen? Interactional synchrony can have long-lasting effects over time. If you're married to someone, and you get along with them more often than not, there's likely going to be a lot of mirroring in that relationship. This kind of mirroring between partners is going to happen for years and years and years. Eventually, when one partner smiles in a certain way, the partner's smile will match. They get similar lines, similar creases, and similar patterns of behavior due to that kind of repetition.

Oculesics

We now arrive at what Shakespeare called the "windows of the soul." Nonverbal communication through the eyes is known as **oculesics**. Technically, oculesics is a form of kinesics because it communicates through movement, but, it's so specific and nuanced, it's worth talking about on its own.

Eye contact has a powerful effect, and we tend to take it for granted. If you were to sit back and watch two people talking, one person, either the talker or the listener, will make more eye contact. It's not something we think about, but when we change who's doing what, it makes a big difference. Usually, the listener is the one that makes the most eye contact. They may also nod and utter verbal cues of agreement.

The speaker, on the other hand, though they also make direct eye contact, will look away every so often to collect their thoughts or to remember something. If you think this difference is subtle or doesn't make that much of a difference, try flipping it around the next time you're talking to someone. If you're the speaker, don't break eye contact. Stay locked on and see how weird and uncomfortable that gets fast, or vice versa. If you're the listener, try making insufficient contact and looking away all the time. The effects are felt quickly.

Pupil dilation is fun to look at because it is an involuntary movement. The pupil will contract whenever our eyes are exposed to bright lights and dilate, or expand, whenever we enter a dark space. It's not just in response to light. Our pupils will contract or dilate based on whether we see something we like. This is why many poker players will often wear sunglasses, even inside, so their pupils won't give away their hand.

Pupil dilation also happens whenever we see a *person* we like. When people retouch pictures of models, they dilate the pupils in Photoshop to create the illusion that the models like the viewer. This nudges passing customers to unconsciously feel a bit more comfort with that picture, and therefore, that store or brand. Check it out next time you're walking around the mall.

Proxemics

Proxemics is nonverbal communication through distance. There's a weird, unconscious thing we do all the time. Think about when you go to a restaurant, and you sit down at the table at the restaurant. What's the first thing you do when you sit down at the table? It's a nonverbal ritual that we do before we order, before we even look at the menu. When we sit down, *we claim territory* by moving cutlery and generally getting situated in a way that carves out our own personal bubble.

This is fascinating to observe at coffee shops too. There's often a long table where people work, and they will carve out little bubbles of space. Bags and laptops mark these boundaries. It feels like that spot is taken even if no one is sitting there. That's proxemics in action.

It's not just space that we claim. Sometimes we can even claim people as territory. Oftentimes, heart-shaped jewelry is usually a gift from a romantic partner claiming territory. Another example might be engagement bands or wedding rings, tattoos, or guys who wear their girlfriends' scrunchies on their wrist. These are all different kinds of territory markers. Back in the 60s, there was a researcher by the name of Ed Hall who was the first one to start analyzing our bubbles.[37] We don't just walk around with a singular personal bubble. We actually walk around with four different bubbles.

The first bubble is called the **intimate zone**, which extends anywhere from physical contact out to about a foot and a half. That's the closest bubble we have to us. Very few people cross into the intimate zone. It's usually saved for significant others or BFFs.

Next is the **personal zone**, which extends anywhere from a foot and a half out to about four feet. This one gets a bit more traffic. We might stand in circles while talking with our friends or include them in the personal zone when sharing a meal.

The **social zone** gets a lot of traffic, which is the next bubble. The social zone goes from about four feet to 12 feet. Most people we interact with are somewhere in our social zone.

The last zone is the **public zone**, which is for strangers. We're not interacting with these people. That extends 12 feet and outward. If you watch strangers at the mall pass each other, you can observe the boundaries of the public zone. Unless space constrains them, they do not pass each other shoulder to shoulder. All things being equal, people will often give each other this little bubble of about 12 feet. They'll curve around each other in space to allow these bubbles to bounce off each other.

These zones are fun to observe when examining family cultures that greet each other with a kiss to the cheek. One of the first things many families do at a family get-together is we go in to do the little kiss on the cheek for aunties. As soon as we kiss them on the cheek, we bounce out to whatever zone with which we are most comfortable. If you're watching your cousins and your friends at a family get-together, you can see which aunties are their favorite because they're going to keep within the personal zone as opposed to bouncing back to the social zone.

Haptics

The last body code is **haptics**, or communication through touch. It's important to note that touch has many different kinds of functions. For example, getting punched in the face is going to tell us a lot about that relationship. A hug, a high five, a handshake, and more are all different examples of haptic communication. In the 70s, five main types of touch were identified.[38] These are especially precise indicators for different boundaries of intimacy in the relationship with someone.

For example, the most distant form of haptic communication is referred to as **Functional-Professional** touch. This kind of touch doesn't serve as a commentary on the relationship. In other words, it's just touch between people because it is their job to touch you in a very specific function. If you book a massage, and the person touches your back, it's because it's their job to give you that massage. It's not because you two are BFFs. If you go to the doctor, and they touch you to listen to your breathing, your heart, or to gauge your range of movement, it's because it is part of their job.

Social-Polite touch is much more common. This touch extends a little bit of goodwill. It's an acknowledgement of another person, like when you meet someone for the first time, and you give them a handshake. During the pandemic it was fascinating to see how we made strides to preserve the relational messages of social-politeness while trying to remove handshakes. We used more fist-bumps or elbow bumps in an effort to maintain the social goodwill we were used to sharing haptically while also reducing the handshakes that once served that function. "Life," as Ian Malcom said, "finds a way."[39]

The next type of touch is **Friendship-Warmth**. This occurs when you see your friends, and you hug them. Or maybe you do that thing guys do that's kind of a handshake but not a handshake, with the interlocked hands. The 'sup thing. It's kind of a half high-five, half handshake, and sometimes you go in for the shoulder bump. That's a form of touch that signals a closer form of friendship than a traditional handshake.

The next type of touch is **Love-Intimacy**. This is always interesting to observe in brand new couples: holding hands when they're walking around, kissing, or one wrapping one's arm around the other's shoulder. You can somewhat tell when a couple has gone from just kind of dating or being casual to now being a couple because they use more haptic communication that suggests love and intimacy.

The last type of touch is **Sexual** touch. In general terms, this refers to touching parts of the body that would be covered by a swimsuit. For a long time, this has been an especially uncomfortable part of haptic communication because, in dating and romance, there was not a lot of explicit verbal consent beyond haptic communication. If you thought your relationship was at the right stage, either you'd go for a sexual touch or you wouldn't. Because there wasn't much verbal communication, we had to start creating campaigns like "No Means No." The problem with the "No Means No" campaign was so long as there wasn't an explicit "no," it could still be interpreted as an unspoken "yes." Now there's a campaign called, "Yes Means Yes" where the only thing that means "yes" is an explicit verbal "yes." For a long time, the only vocabulary we had for the most intimate type of touch had been haptics, but if we only rely on haptic communication, there will be a lot of miscommunication and boundary issues. Thankfully, the normalization of explicit consent is helping to restore boundaries. Practice using verbal yeses and communicating enthusiastically with your partner so you can gain the full benefit of this specific form of haptic communication.

One of my favorite studies about haptics is from 1984 (the year, not the book). If you hang around enough psychology courses, you are bound to hear about the Midas Touch study. For this experiment, researchers recruited servers at different restaurants.[40] In one condition, the servers would bring the check at the end of the meal, drop it on the table, and say, "Thanks for coming. Hope to see you again next time." In the second condition, the servers would drop the check off, lightly touch the customer's arm somewhere between the shoulder and the elbow, and say, "Thanks for coming. Hope to see you again next time." The group who did the slight touch earned more tips than the servers who didn't. The touch suggested interpersonal warmth, sending a relational message that there was goodwill toward the customer, which was reciprocated with a higher tip. A slight touch communicated that the server wasn't just some random person but a fellow human like the customer.

These are the four different body codes: **kinesics**, **oculesics**, **proxemics**, and **haptics**. Next up, are going to be the four different contextual codes, that is, nonverbal communication that you can't even see in the body no matter how hard you look.

To continue our discussion of nonverbal communication, we now turn to communication without words that also have nothing to do with the body. You couldn't see these forms of nonverbal communication in a body even if you were looking for them. We're going to discuss four different kinds of contextual codes, which are **vocalics**, **environments**, **chronemics**, and **olfactics**. Now, same as before, if any of these look like they've got some hidden words in them that seem familiar, it's probably true. **Vocalics** contains the word "vocal" and refers to nonverbal communication through the voice. **Environments** simply refers to our surroundings (you'll never walk into a room the same way after we talk about nonverbal communication through environments). **Chronemics**, kind of like "chrono" or chronology, is nonverbal communication through time. Last but not least, is **olfactics**, nonverbal communication through smell.

Vocalics

Communication through voice is usually imagined as speaking words, but that's not necessarily all there is. If somebody tries to interrupt a group conversation by clearing their throat, that's vocalic information, even though no words were spoken. There are many different things that vocalics can do, such as **repetition**, which reinforces information being communicated verbally. When you make an affirmative noise such as "uh huh" to indicate you're still listening, that's an example of repetition through vocalics.

Accenting works by stressing different words in the sentence. You can completely change the meaning of a sentence this way. For example, in the sentence "I never said she stole my wallet," there are seven words. The sentence could have seven different meanings depending on what word you choose to accent. "**I** never said she stole my wallet." What's that mean? Somebody said she stole my wallet, but it wasn't me. "I never said **she** stole my wallet." Now it means that yes, I said somebody stole my wallet, but she didn't do it. "I never said she stole my ***wallet***." She stole something, but she didn't steal my wallet (she stole my heart). Accenting can completely change the meaning of a sentence even though that sentence is the same verbally.

The third function is **substitution**, which occurs when you completely replace verbal information all together. If you have ever seen *Wall-E* or *Star Wars*, there's a lot of vocalic information in those movies. The beloved R2-D2 never says a single word, but you always know what's on R2's mind. For the entirety of the movie, he only speaks through various robot noises with beeps and boops, but you know exactly what he is thinking, feeling, and saying. Fast, high-pitched beeps are contributions like excitement or surprise. Slow, drawn-out, lower pitched *booooops* are for a sad R2. For a more human example, if you're given bad news, and you respond *ugh*, that's a vocalic response substituting a verbal one.

Regulation refers to guiding the conversation's flow. Clearing one's throat to enter a conversation is an example of regulation. Regulating occurs whenever we claim the floor, or we yield the floor to someone else. If you want to hand the floor off to a more introverted coworker in a meeting, your sentence might slow down towards the end and have a rising inflection. "So, that's where our lead generation stands for Q3, but I think Jen has some ideas for next month...?"

The final function of vocalics is **contradiction**. This is a fun one because it's basically like sarcasm. Let's say someone announces that a meeting is going to be on a video call instead of in person. Some people might say, "That's great!" They'd be happy because they prefer to work from home. Other people say, "That's...*great*..." but they don't actually think it's great. In the example, we have two verbally identical responses, but nonverbally very, very different because the vocalic information completely changes. Contradiction is a bit like accenting, but instead of changing the meaning of the sentence to any one of a number of possibilities based on which word we stress, contradiction delivers the precise opposite of whatever meaning is suggested by the words.

Vocalics wields huge influence in the way our messages are conveyed to each other. They could be repeating, accenting, substituting, regulating, or contradicting. This can show up in text messages or in writing. Long pauses can be conveyed with the little ellipsis symbol, an exclamation as all caps, bold, or italics. All of that added punctuation and font style is us finding ways to translate vocalic information into written form.

One of my favorite examples of this in writing is a sentence designed firstly to anger all the ladies reading this and then to anger all the guys. It's the same sentence, I'm only going to change the vocalic information, not the verbal information. Here's the sentence.

A woman without her man is nothing.

"Boo!" "Hiss!" "Shame!" I understand. It's not a nice sentence. Punctuation, though, can change the meaning completely. Let's add some vocalic information by adding just a couple deliberate pauses.

A woman: without her, man is nothing.

Oooh...That's a *very* different sentence. And yet, the sentence is identical, at least verbally. All it takes is a couple of pauses in the right place, and the sentence's meaning flips to the complete opposite.

Be aware of the way your vocalic information shapes your interactions with people. Is the inflection rising towards the end of the sentence like a question? Is the inflection dropping down to speak with conviction? What's the volume like? What's the speed and pacing like? The cadence, the rhythm, of what we say all have huge impacts on the way we interact with people.

Environments

Casinos are perfect examples of very specifically controlled environments. If you ever walk into a Las Vegas casino, you hear bells, whistles, ringing, beeping, and coins jingling. It's the sound of victory! Somewhere someone is winning something. There are flashing lights and colors. It's exciting and vibrant. It's designed to be interesting and appealing. So, you go in and drop off a nickel. But if you start paying close attention, you look around at the walls. There are no clocks on the walls of the casinos in Vegas. There are also very few windows, if any at all, to the outside world. Doors are usually very far away so you can't even see outside, which means it's very hard to track the passage of time. Once we get lured in by the vibrant colors and all the ringing noises, we don't know how long we spend at the slot machines just dropping in nickel after nickel. All the servers will bring people free drinks to keep them comfortable and gambling some more. They're pumping extra oxygen in the casinos to help keep people awake and alert. It's a very controlled environment.

Let's get all Sherlock Holmes-y and scrutinize our surroundings by examining nonverbal communication through

environments. The psychologist, Sam Gosling, published a book called *Snoop*.[41] One of the interesting concepts he introduces is the idea of identity claims. According to Gosling, the things we keep around us in a room like pictures, trophies, little artifacts, souvenirs, can be categorized as two different sorts of identity claims.

More specifically, an **identity claim** is anything that speaks about the character of the owner. For example, let's say I got a tennis trophy. The trophy reminds me I'm a good tennis player, that I'm a hard worker. If there's a picture of my family, then it reminds me I'm a family person. This is what's important in life. What Gosling noticed is that certain artifacts are meant for certain *audiences*. For example, a **self-oriented identity claim** is any object left in a room whose audience is the owner, like my trophy. If, however, the audience is somebody else, like a visitor or a sibling or a friend, someone not the owner, then it is an **other-oriented identity claim**.

For example, if you walk into your boss's office, and there's a picture of their family on the desk, Gosling would have you notice if the photograph is facing towards the boss or towards you. The direction of the photo indicates its function. If that photograph is facing towards the owner, the boss, it's a self-oriented identity claim. That photo is there to remind the boss about how much they love their family, what their work is all about.

However, if the photo is facing towards you, then it is an other-oriented identity claim. An other-oriented identity claim is any object whose function is to communicate something about the owner to others. The boss is showing you their family. The boss is communicating to you they are a warm person who loves their family. The photo isn't a reminder for themselves, it's a way to let you into their world. If you walk into somebody's house, and they point out their tennis trophy, that's probably an other-oriented identity claim. It's a conversation piece. However, if they have their trophy in their bedroom, where, for example, you could only see it if you were lying in their bed, then it's a self-oriented identity claim.

While you can learn a lot from little items and objects, you can also go bigger than that. We call larger-scale environments **sociopetal** or **sociofugal** environments.

A **sociopetal** (pronounced SO-see-OP-ettul) environment is any environment that facilitates communication and makes it easy to interact with people. If you walk into a coffee shop, and several couches form an L-shape in the corner, it is easy for people to sit around there and talk. They sit around with their friends, they hang out, they talk, tell stories, and then they go grab another cup of coffee.

A **sociofugal** (SO-see-oh-FYU-gull) environment is any environment that is not conducive to communication. It inhibits communication. For example, the seats on an airplane are very sociofugal. It's hard to talk to people on an airplane. You might be able to talk to the person directly next to you, but with that hard right angle, you have to stretch your neck, and it's really uncomfortable. You definitely can't have a conversation with your friend two rows up. Think of a classroom on test day where all the desks are separated from each other, facing the front of the room. That's a very sociofugal environment. You don't want to facilitate communication during test-taking time because that defeats the purpose of the test. But if you want collaboration and people talking in a classroom, say for a group project, then putting all the desks in a big circle can encourage that kind of discussion because everyone gets a front-row seat. Everyone has a direct line-of-sight to everyone else in the room.

You can use your knowledge of sociopetal and sociofugal spaces strategically too. Let's say you're going to a big dinner party, and maybe you're trying to break the ice a bit more, be more of a life of the party, trying to talk to more people while you're there. If you think about a classically shaped rectangular table, where do we usually put the guest of honor? At the head of the table, even though that position is very sociofugal. If you're at the head of the table, you can't interact with very many people. People can see you, but you can't talk to them.

The real sociopetal position on the table, if you're trying to get to know people, is to sit in the middle because that gives you a direct line of sight and a short distance between you and a lot of other people there. If you imagine people on your left and right, if they wanted to talk to each other, they'd have to talk through you, so you become part of that conversation too. So, if you want to honor the VIP at a birthday party, don't put them at the head of the table. Put them in the middle, right in the center at a very sociopetal position.

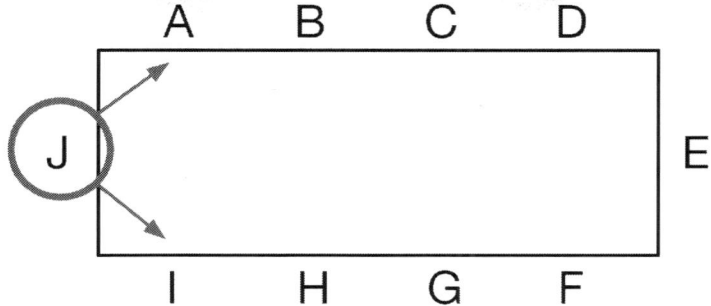

The head of the table (like J) is very sociofugal

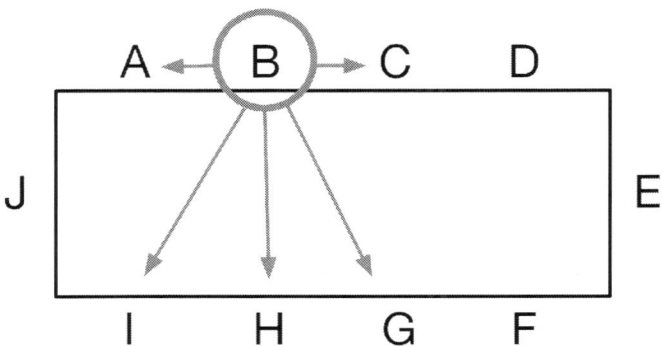

A side seat (like B) is very sociopetal

Vice versa, if you're going to a dinner party, and you don't want to be there, you just want to bury your head in the sand and wait for all of it to end, then you probably want to make sure you get a sociofugal spot at the table. You want to pick a corner of the table because that's going to have a line of sight with maybe one or two other people. But really, the rest of the table is blocked off if you're in that sociofugal position.

If you look around and see artifacts are shaping the interactions, then you can learn more about the people around you. Are they self-oriented identity claims or other-oriented identity claims? Is the seating area sociopetal, conducive to communication? Is it sociofugal, designed to inhibit communication? That's going to give you a huge insight into how people will behave in their environments and how you might be able to change those variables to your benefit. That's a quick look at nonverbal communication through environments. Up next, the most invisible nonverbal communication of all. We'll take a look at nonverbal communication through time, otherwise known as **chronemics.**

Chronemics

Think about waiting time. It can have a huge influence on our interactions. Waiting can make things feel very awkward or very efficient. We can feel very cared for or very neglected just through chronemic communication. For example, chronemics is one of the most common ways people communicate power distance to each other. Power distance has to do with who's in charge: who's the boss, who's the employee; who's the leader, who's the follower. So, one of the ways you can see subordination and dominance communicated through chronemics is with wait time. Think about who usually makes the other person wait. Is it the boss who makes the employee wait or is it the employee who makes the boss wait?

Usually, it's the boss who makes the employee wait. Those in a position of power can create wait time. If you show up for a job interview, then you're usually the one in the waiting area, waiting for the boss to be ready, for the interviewer to come and see you, not the other way around. Although there is a way you can close this perceived gap of power distance. If you ever show up, and you know you're going to wait for someone, try the following: bring something to do. Of course, I don't mean you should be on your phone playing games. We need to be doing something productive for the purpose of this exercise. It will seem like your time isn't at the behest of someone else. If you're actively doing something, then it closes that perceived power gap created by wait time.

Chronemic communication is especially easy to see in the 21st century. Now that we live in an age of digital communication with email, social media posts, and text messages, we encounter wait time far more often than we ever used to. Even waiting for someone to text you back—that's chronemic communication.

Norms are going to differ from person to person and from relationship to relationship, but suppose you're texting a friend, and you are accustomed to about a minute wait for a response. You ask them if they want to see a movie, and a minute later they reply, "sure." Chances are, you feel like they probably want to watch a movie. Very normal interaction. Let's pretend that instead of a minute, it takes them forty-five minutes to text the same "sure." Now it feels like that person doesn't want to see a movie that much.

We can give them the benefit of the doubt, right? Maybe they were in the shower, maybe they were driving, or maybe their phone died. But, rightly or wrongly, it *feels* like a different interaction. The wait time shapes the relational message.

Unconsciously, it doesn't seem like they're very interested, whether that's true or not.

Longer wait time for a response feels less urgent. The quicker response feels more urgent, more receptive to the message. This gets even more complicated when you start adding in other elements of nonverbal communication to your texting. Remember how we can add vocalics to text with punctuation? What if someone adds an ellipsis to their affirmative? Suppose you text the invite to your friend and one minute later the response is "...sure." Now it doesn't feel so urgent. It probably feels like they are reluctant. Or maybe your friend sends an affirmative with an exclamation point, "sure!" Their vocalics make them seem excited. There could also be some kinesics added in because nowadays we can add facial expressions to text messages thanks to emoticons and emojis. What if you invite your friend to a movie and they respond, "...sure. ;)" That feels like a *very* different conversation! That's more like saying yeah, let's watch a movie—and whatever happens...happens...

> *wanna see a movie?*
> Normal: *sure*
> Reluctant: *...sure*
> Excited: *sure!*
> [redacted]: *...sure ;)*

Olfactics

This one is extremely invisible because it has to do with smell. **Olfactics** is nonverbal communication using smell. This may sound kind of strange, but if you woke up this morning, and you decided deliberately to put on some specific smell of deodorant, you have decided to communicate olfactically. Although, I suppose if you woke up this morning, and you defiantly decided *not* to put on deodorant, you're communicating something else olfactically too. Speaking of deodorants, it's interesting how scents themselves communicate things. We're very picky about what scent we use on ourselves because it's going to communicate something about us. For example, one of the easiest ways we communicate things through smell is gender.

There are very feminine deodorant smells like the fruity stuff, the flowery stuff, the green apple shampoos, or the jasmine field flower things. All these natural floral scents are saved for the ladies, which is weird because then for guys, there's not a whole lot of nice smelling things leftover. At least, few that are real. The next time you ever go into the deodorant section of the store, look at the guys' smells. They're nonsense. They make up a bunch of gibberish. It's like "Arctic Steel," "Ocean Force," or whatever. Just dumb made-up junk because they have to sound intense and masculine. But smells don't care what's feminine or what's masculine, only our culture does.

Researchers in 2003 got interested in how our perceptions of each other can be shaped by smell.[42] A bunch of guys were recruited, given plain white t-shirts and odorless soap, and were asked to wear the shirts to bed for a week. By the end of the week, the shirts had been nice and saturated with their natural...man musk. When the shirts were returned, they were put into individual boxes without any identifying features, so you couldn't judge the shirt based on its size or what color it was. The researchers invited some women and asked them to sniff each box. They then needed to tell the researchers which shirt they liked best.

Each woman gave a rating for how nice or bad it smelled. It turned out the shirts the women liked the best belonged to men they found most physically attractive. The women could *smell* the hot guys.

One of the ways the researchers were able to measure the guys' attractiveness was via symmetry. It's hard to measure attractiveness because it's so subjective. The guys with the nicest smelling shirts tended to be more symmetrical. The left side of their bodies looked more like the right side of their bodies. Pretty cool. Of course, researchers wanted to know what happened if we flipped it around. So, they did the same routine of doling out plain white shirts to women. Guys took some sniffs, and the same thing happened. The ones they thought smelled the best belonged to women they found most attractive.

There was an interesting secondary finding. Shirts that guys thought smelled the best tended to belong to ovulating women. In other words, they were at the most fertile part of their mensural cycle. Of course, this wasn't a one-to-one, ESP-like detection. Guys didn't sniff the shirt and say, "Bingo! She's good to go!" But the average ratings for smell tended to reveal a statistical pattern.

Another interesting finding we attribute to olfactics is that couples tend to find a partner who has a complimentary *major histocompatibility complex* or MHC. The MHC has to do with our immune system and the kinds of hormones that allow us to have a stronger resistance to certain diseases and viruses. It's a fancy way of saying we tend to find a partner who is immune to things we are not immune to. We cover each other's weaknesses.

There's no guarantee everyone always finds a partner with a complimentary MHC, but it's a real finding. It's not just pheromones for lions and tigers and bears. It's also us. Oh my. Apart from communication, smell also has some interesting unconscious impacts on people's behavior. A slight whiff of a lemon-scented cleaner, like a Lysol spray, in a room will encourage people to tidy up, arrange books neatly, and pick up after themselves.[43] Even if you bring the Lysol scent level down so low they can't smell it consciously, they still tend to tidy up more. Pretty neat.

We have talked a lot about nonverbal communication. There are body codes which include **kinesics**, nonverbal communication through movement, such as facial expressions, hand gestures, gait, and interactional synchrony, like mirroring. **Oculesics** is nonverbal communication through the eyes, such as eye contact or pupil dilation. **Proxemics** is nonverbal communication through distance, such as our personal bubbles or zones. **Haptics** is nonverbal communication through touch.

Then there are contextual codes. **Vocalics** is nonverbal communication through the voice, such as volume, cadence, rhythm, and speech rate. For **environments**, look for different kinds of identity claims, whether they're self or other-oriented. There are also sociopetal and sociofugal environments, use them intentionally to get people talking or to quiet down. In the case of **chronemics**, nonverbal communication through time, wait time can create subordination and dominance. You can also consider how chronemics creates a sense of urgency through asynchronous communication like text messages or emails. Finally, **olfactics** is nonverbal communication through smell. We realize now that certain people can smell attraction in their partners, and that over time, we tend to find someone with a compatible immune system to us, not because of anything we can see or hear, but presumably through things we can smell, even if unconsciously.

10 Tips on Nonverbal Communication

1. Send the relational messages you choose, not the ones you leave to chance

We send two messages: content and relational. Your relational message (e.g., interest, fondness, annoyance, boredom, etc.) is almost entirely nonverbal. Since you constantly send relational messages anyway, you may as well do so intentionally.

2. Be forgiving of the indelicate relational messages others send you

Other people won't always be aware of their own relational messages. They may seem gruff, terse, or disinterested with you even if they bear no ill-will. Save some patience for them.

3. Use mirroring to check your "Rapport Thermometer"

Do you and the other person have interactional synchrony? That's an indicator the conversation is going well.

4. Walk with posture and purpose

Relax your shoulders, straighten your back, lead with your chest. Walk like you have somewhere to be. You're going to walk anyway. You may as well walk with purpose.

5. Make appropriate eye contact as a speaker or a listener

As a speaker, try not to bore into the brain of your listener with too much eye contact. As a listener, try not to neglect the speaker with insufficient eye contact. Some of us struggle with this more than others, and that's okay so long as we try our best.

6. Claim or release territory

Set up nonverbal boundaries of personal space if you want more room. If you realize you have an excess, move your stuff to make room for others.

7. Mind your tone

The way our voice *sounds* can often have *more* impact than the *words* we use.

8. Read the room (literally)

Take a look at the rooms you're in. What items are other-oriented? What do you think they are meant to communicate to visitors? What items are self-oriented? What do you think they reinforce for the owner?

9. Create Sociopetal and Sociofugal spaces on purpose

Want people to talk? Arrange chairs or couches in semi-circles or L-shaped corners with 90-degree angles. Want to stop people from talking? Arrange all the chairs facing the same way.

10. Be mindful of response times

Waiting time for texts or emails, whether intentional or not, can shape perceptions of the conversation. Be aware of these perceptions at the very least. Shape them on purpose, at best.

PART II: Public Discourse

Public discourse is the ongoing societal discussion of everything. It includes talking heads on cable news, online petitions your friends want you to sign, politicians debating on TV, awkward topics we try to avoid at Thanksgiving dinners, waving protest signs on sidewalks, and old high school acquaintances posting (totally well-informed) opinions on social media. The topics of our discourse cover celebrity gossip, the Middle East, bad movie castings, vaccines, elections, and all manner of spicy topics that divide opinions. But whatever the specific topic, the aim of our public discourse is determining what people should *do*. You should vote for _____ for President, X actor should break up with Y actor, healthcare should be publicly funded, and HBO should redo the final season of *Game of Thrones* are all topics that have entered our public discourse, and they are all about what people should do.

As a crafter of communication, it will be vital for you to have principles you can employ in all kinds of conversations, debates, and persuasive appeals as you navigate public discourse. How are we going to tackle every single topic and disagreement? Well, we won't. We can't. That's beyond the scope of this book. But the Pareto Principle, also called the 80/20 Principle, suggests we don't have to learn *everything* to have remarkable results. We can focus on a few vitally important ideas. The principle suggests that roughly 20% of inputs are responsible for 80% of the output.[44] For example:

- About 80% of your happiness comes from the same 20% of people in your life
- Around 80% of the money you spend on restaurants goes to the same 20% of places you visit
- If you play an instrument, roughly 80% of your music will use the same 20% of chords you know
- In business, roughly 80% of your revenue will come from the same 20% of customers that buy from you

This is a rough ratio that is not a strict rule of the universe, but it's an interesting trend with a useful takeaway: you can derive huge benefit by focusing on the vital few things that matter most and ignoring everything else. You could go from knowing nothing about music to competently playing a huge number of songs if you just learn the 20% of chords you will use the most. In fact, author Josh Kaufman does just this by learning only four chords on the ukulele and then playing an impressive musical medley on a TEDx stage.[45]

If we could find the smallest number of *ideas* that play a vital role in the largest number of *disagreements*, then we can dramatically improve our ability to competently navigate any kind of dispute, argument, or debate in public discourse. So, what principles apply to just about every kind of disagreement? What are the "four chords" of public discourse?

To identify them, we first need to dissect disagreements. There are three different types of issues that ground all disagreements: **fact, value,** and **policy.**

An issue of fact is a dispute about what's true or what's false. An issue of value is a dispute over what is good or bad. An issue of policy is about what we should do or not do. Let's take climate change as an example.

An **issue of fact** would be "Human activity causes global warming." It is either true that human activity contributes to a change in global temperature or it is false. This is not a matter of opinion because it doesn't matter what anyone personally believes. Even if none of us believed it, carbon dioxide would still go on trapping heat (or it would not). As science fiction author Philip K. Dick put it, "Reality is that which, when you stop believing in it, doesn't go away." The answer to an issue of fact does not hinge on what anyone thinks—it is objectively true or false.

Whatever beliefs we adopt as true or false might then bring us to debate an **issue of value**. Issues of value are ultimately all about establishing what is good or bad. There are a million ways something can be good and a million ways something can be bad. Something might be "good" because it's described as *useful, moral, beautiful, interesting, inspiring*, or—as the kids say—*lit*. On the other hand, something might be bad because it's *harmful, overrated, boring, immoral*, or *directed by Zack Snyder* (okay, that last one is technically a claim of fact because either a movie *is* or *is not* directed by Snyder, but still—you get it). Our value-based opinions might sound like "Global warming is the most *urgent* issue facing humanity" while another may be "Global warming is *not as concerning* as the media makes it out to be." But what is "urgent"? What counts as "concerning" or not? These are not objective descriptions; they are subjective evaluations. They are issues of value.

Issues of policy appear around climate change too. Issues of policy are disputes over what we should do or do not do. We should start doing *this*, we should stop doing *that*. Policies invoke action or prohibition. They are not about what's objectively true or false. They are not about what's subjectively good or bad. They are about the actions we ought to take or not take. An issue of policy might sound like "Governments should offer tax credits for using renewable energy."

At some level, all disagreements are about what is *true*, what is *good*, or what we should be *doing*.

Topic	Issue of Fact (True or False)	Issue of Value (Good or Bad)	Issue of Policy (Do or Do Not)
Climate change	*Global temperature rise is the result of human activity.*	*Climate change is an urgent problem.*	*Governments should offer tax credits for renewable energy production.*
Genetically Modified Organisms	*GMO crops lead to greater produce yields.*	*GMOs are an effective tool in combatting world hunger.*	*Governments should subsidize GMO research.*
Kids	*Our family makes enough money to sustain a child.*	*Our family makes enough money to give a child a happy life.*	*Our family should have a child.*
Steve	*Steve eats other people's lunch from the fridge.*	*Steve is the worst.*	*Steve should be promoted to Director of Sales.*

Public discourse largely deals with issues of policy (e.g., vote for/legalize/fund/ban/require _____); after all, policies make up politics. Even if you have no interest in the subject of politics, you will be a participant in disputes of policy at home and at work. A couple deciding whether to have a child, a business deciding how to allocate surplus funds, a family choosing a vacation destination, and a committee deciding which candidate to hire are all dealing with issues of policy.

But issues of policy hinge on our stances on issues of value. What a person thinks should be *done* depends on what they think is good. What a person thinks is *good* depends on what they think is true. Issues of fact, value, and policy are all interconnected. Even though our most visible disputes are issues of policy, to improve our discussions of policy we need to have vital, reliable principles to first decide what is true and what is good.

Part II of this book will give you these tools. Chapter 6 reveals fundamental ideas we use for figuring out what is true or false, from medicine to conspiracy theories. Chapter 7 covers vital principles we use for deciding what things are right or wrong. I won't presume to tell you what things in this world *are* right or wrong, but I do hope to reveal the underlying principles that others use—whether they know it or not—when they decide what's right and wrong. Understanding these hidden principles will give you more patience for others who seem blatantly wrong, give you ways of convincing others of your ideas, and tools for self-correction when you might be in the wrong without realizing it.

While this book can't cover every idea you will ever need for every disagreement about what to do, we can at least look at the vital few principles that drive issues of fact and issues of value. These tools will, in turn, help you navigate disagreements about what we should do.

Chapter 6

Talk About What's True

"The first principle is that you must not fool yourself—and you are the easiest person to fool."

— Richard Feynman

How do we know what's true? How do we know what's false? It's a heavy problem, and yet we take it for granted. If I asked you to make a list of facts you know, that would be pretty easy, right? I know my name is Chris. I know the sky is blue. I know I am writing this book. I know I'm on Earth. I know one plus one equals two. That's a quick list of facts I know. But how do I know these things? And more importantly, how do I know that I know them?

Epistemology is a branch of philosophy which is all about how we know what we know. We're not going to have to go entirely into philosophy, but there are a few concepts worth knowing for any of us as we enter disagreements, especially when trying to figure out what's true. This is important so we can analyze evidence, avoid conspiracies, and come up with the most accurate possible version of what is real.

The concepts presented here are a framework that can be helpful in discerning fact from fiction. We need to run through a few questions we easily take for granted. For example, how can we actually *know* things to be true? Once we have a collection of what things could be true, how do we know which ones to *believe*? If we have a big collection of facts, where does evidence *come from*? Once we have a collection of credible facts, how do we *explain* the evidence we find? After all, facts don't speak for themselves. A bunch of dinosaur bones in the ground could mean that life evolved over time through natural selection, or it could mean aliens put them there as a prank.

These concepts will help you vet your own information, your evidence for a debate, or any stories that cross your social media feed. How do you vet the information that crosses your path? If you hear a story from a friend or a family member, or see it on the news, how can you vet the information that gets presented to you in your own life? That's what we'll be discussing. Let's start off with the first concept.

Solipsism: What do we really know?

We want to begin by asking the following question: what do we know is true? And I mean, *really Know*, like with a capital K. Well, certainly, you know your name. You know you are on

TALK ABOUT WHAT'S TRUE   149

Earth. You know you are reading this book. You know the sky is blue. You know one plus one equals two. Right?

You might remember a disagreement that took place on the Internet years ago. It was about a photograph that divided households, ruined friendships, and tested relationships. The picture was of *The Dress*.[46] No one could agree what color the dress was. Was it blue and black? Was it white and gold? No one could agree. You might remember the dress. Give it a quick Google and reignite the debate with your loved ones. It took the world by storm, and it forced people to confront the fact their eyes didn't necessarily agree with their friends' eyes. This dress might be blue and black. It might be white and gold, but surely whatever colors you see, you'll believe that you are right. In your opinion, the other people couldn't possibly see a different color. Our eyes can give us information that is different from reality. Our *ears* might even give us different information. Remember "yanny" and "laurel"? Give them a search. If we can't trust our senses, how do we know what's real?

This was an important question explored by French philosopher René Descartes. Descartes wanted to list down on paper all the things he could know with *absolute* certainty. If there was any *possibility* he could doubt a fact, it would not make his list. He couldn't write down the sky is blue because eyes can be tricked. In fact, he couldn't put down *anything* that was learned by way of sight. What else is learned by sight? Lots of things. He couldn't write down grass is green, dogs have four legs, or birds fly. He couldn't even put down his family members' names because it's possible his ears were deceived. Remember, if there was a possibility of doubt, it didn't make the list. Eventually, he realized that any knowledge gleaned through the five senses couldn't be relied on with complete certainty.

Descartes, realizing he couldn't trust his senses, turned to math. Math is pure and true and exists entirely unto itself. After all, math doesn't depend on how people perceive it. One plus one equals two. Every time. Right?

But... Descartes wondered, what if I've been deceived? What if he had gone mad or there were some mischievous demon playing tricks on his mind? If that were the case, then even Descartes' own sense of mathematical logic would be *"merely the delusions of dreams which he has devised to ensnare my judgement. I shall consider myself as not having hands or eyes, or flesh, or blood or senses, but as falsely believing that I have all these things."* If there was even a possibility of doubt, then it didn't make the list. While he might think that one plus one is two, it could have actually been fourteen the whole time. Even math couldn't make the list of things that Descartes could know with absolute certainty.

As you can imagine, this was a pretty strange experience. We're not really left with much else. I can't even know if my friends exist. I can't know the sky is blue. I can't know math is consistent. What is there? Well, Descartes actually did end up finding one thing he could put on the list. He put down that he exists. Why? Because he was thinking, even if he was nuts. He was able to jot down "cogito ergo sum" or as you have famously heard it, "I think, therefore I am."[47] Literally, the one thing he knew with absolute certainty was that he existed.

Maybe everyone you know is a hallucination. Maybe this is all a simulation. Maybe you're the only thing that exists. Wow. We're starting off heavy. The idea that the only thing you can know for certain is your existence is called *solipsism*, and it's still hotly up for debate in philosophy. My goal isn't to make you a solipsist. I don't want to convince you everything is an illusion, but it's worth thinking about because it reveals a fundamental principle as we try to determine what's real.

When we ask ourselves how we know what's true, we need to start by making a pretty big concession: we cannot know things with absolute certainty. We just can't know. The best that we can do is infer, which is to arrive at the best possible conclusion. We use whatever evidence and reason are available to us, and then we make our inference. This is the first fundamental principle to know as you enter any kind of disagreement over what is true: *we cannot know something with absolute certainty, we just make the best possible inference.*

Of course, not all inferences are created equally. For example, while I can't know with certainty I am human, I infer that I am. Is my inference that I'm a human being just as valid as the inference that I'm a polar bear made of cotton candy, tricked into believing he's a human? No. But why not? If we can't know things with absolute certainty, how come some inferences might be better than others? We need a tool to help us discern *which* inferences to make.

Bayesian Inference: How do we choose what to believe?

We often think of knowledge in black and white absolutes. We either *know* something or we *do not know* something. A person is *right* or a person is *wrong*. But this tendency to regard knowledge as so categorically right or wrong can mislead us. Once we think we are right we stop investigating. Once we think an idea is wrong, we disregard it. But what if our "right" idea is wrong? Because we stopped investigating, we persist in our error with no way of realizing it. If we discard a correct idea, thinking it was "wrong," then we would never revisit it to discover the truth.

Kathryn Schulz, author of the thought-provoking book *Being Wrong: Adventures in the Margin of Error*, points out that you never experience what it feels like to be wrong.[48] After all, when you're wrong, you think you're right. So being wrong actually feels like being right. You know what it feels like to realize you *were* wrong, but by that time you are no longer wrong. Being wrong is not a feeling you can experience.

We are extremely vulnerable to being wrong because we are quick to devotedly cling to what we feel is "right" (or cast out what we think is "wrong") and because we have no way of experiencing what it feels like to be wrong. This is dangerous. We need a different way of thinking about what is right and wrong. We need to adopt new facts more slowly and revisit rejected facts more often. How can we do that? We need to talk about rodeo clowns.

Was your mom ever a professional rodeo clown? You know the job, the unsung heroes who dress as clowns to distract

TALK ABOUT WHAT'S TRUE 153

rampaging bulls so that cowboys can safely enter and exit the rodeo ring. My guess is your mom was never a rodeo clown—or at least, you *think* she never was.

Suppose one day you are going through some old photographs that you found in a forgotten box that was tucked away in a closet. Among the dusty photos is a picture of your mom at a rodeo, dressed as a professional rodeo clown. What do you think now? Are you now 100% convinced that mom was a professional rodeo clown? Probably not. My guess is the photo would raise more questions for you than answers. You are probably not yet rewriting everything you know about your mom and believing she led a secret life. After all, there are lots of explanations for the photo.

It could be a...

- Secret life—mom *really did* lead a secret life as a rodeo clown

- Costume—mom dressed as a rodeo clown for Halloween one year, it's just never come up in conversation

- Photoshopped prank—for reasons unknown, a tech-proficient relative has photoshopped mom as a rodeo clown

- Doppelganger—the picture is of a real rodeo clown that looks a lot like mom, the family kept the photo for the fun coincidence

- Dream—you aren't even looking at photos, you're asleep

- Case of time travel—since you last spoke to her, mom has gone back in time and lived a new life as a rodeo clown

If we are keeping an open mind like we should, these are all genuine possibilities. And these are only a fraction of the possibilities, you could list an infinite number of other possibilities. That's probably why we aren't convinced with 100% certainty that mom led a secret life. We're not totally convinced, but the possibility is now on our radar. Say that 100% confidence is absolute, unshakeable certainty something is true, and 0% is absolute, unshakable certainty something is false. If we had to rate our confidence for each possibility and rank them from most likely to least likely, it might look something like this.

- Costume – 90% confident mom was in a costume

- Doppelganger – 40% confident the picture is of a look-alike

- Photoshopped prank – 10% confident someone faked this on a computer

- Dream – 5% confident you're asleep

- Secret life – 1% confident mom led a secret life as a rodeo clown

- Case of time travel – 0.0000000001% confident mom time-travelled

Suppose you continue digging through the box and at the bottom is a rodeo clown outfit—it has the same smudges and stains as the costume in the photo. You have found the outfit from the picture. This now eliminates the photoshopped possibility because the outfit wasn't created digitally. How else might the discovery change our confidence in the possibilities?

- Costume – ~~90%~~ 99% confident (you found the costume from the photo)

- Secret life – ~~1%~~ 10% confident (probably not, but I mean, the outfit *does* exist)

- Doppelganger – ~~40%~~ 2% confident (not likely anymore, but maybe the look-alike gave mom the outfit?)

- Photoshopped prank – ~~10%~~ 0.001% confident (the outfit was not created digitally)

- Dream – ~~5%~~ 0.01 confident (you pinched yourself, you're awake)

- Case of time travel – 0.0000000001% confident (we can't completely rule it out—we don't know what we don't know)

Notice how the order of possibilities has changed again. New evidence has changed our confidence, increasing it for some options, decreasing it for others, and eliminating it for a few. Now, technically, we can't *entirely* eliminate options (time travel still *might* be an option). But in the absence of better evidence (like a DeLorean with flaming wheels) let's take the bottom three lowest possibilities, round them down to 0%, and call them "eliminated."

As you inspect the clown outfit, you find, embroidered on the inside of the collar, your mother's name and the official mark of Ringling Bros. and Barnum & Bailey's Clown College. This outfit isn't some cheap costume from your local party store, it's a uniform. It's made from quality, durable materials and only given out to official graduates of rodeo clown training. What might this do to our confidence?

- Secret life – ~~10%~~ 90% confident

- Costume – ~~99%~~ 10% confident

- Doppelganger – ~~2%~~ 0.01% confident

Now, the secret life possibility leapfrogs to the top position. The new evidence you found is a big revelation, but you still don't want to believe it. After all, isn't it possible that mom just wanted a rodeo clown costume that was authentic and custom-made for...some reason? It's possible. Then you check the pocket.

In the pocket is a handwritten letter, in your mom's own distinctive handwriting, reminiscing about the good old days of being a professional rodeo clown and how she would one day keep it all a secret once she had kids. Secret life – 99% confident.

This is what evidence does for us. While keeping an open mind, there are an infinite number of possibilities that could be true. Evidence reduces the range of infinite possibilities to a narrower range of infinite possibilities. Anything could be possible; we must always keep an open mind, but, as the saying goes, "not so open that our brains fall out."[49]

As we collect evidence, different inferences become more likely or less likely. Even if we never reach truth with 100% absolute certainty, we get to a point where there is enough evidence to make an inference which is, as the courts say, "beyond reasonable doubt."

This is how Bayesian inference works. Instead of claiming factual certainty, *claim more or less confidence in facts, constantly adjusting your confidence with the addition of new evidence*. Your "knowledge" (that is, your confident inferences) should always be in a state of flux, ready to be slightly revised as you encounter new evidence.

Knowledge is not black and white; you do not absolutely *know* or *do not know* something (remember the false dichotomy from Chapter 2?). What you have are gradations of grey. You suspect things with more or less confidence. I don't know that I'm a human being writing a book, but based on the available evidence, I suspect that I am (with a high degree of confidence). That's the conclusion I will infer until new evidence to the contrary comes along. By approaching our knowledge with this provisional mindset, we can slow down our tendency to quickly and devotedly cling to what we think is true or to cast out what we are sure is false.

Instead of claiming that something is true or false, think about how *confident* you are that it's true on a scale of 0 (definitely false) to 100 (definitely true). A score of 50 is not knowing either way. For example, if you think that so-and-so politician embezzled money, pause and ask yourself, "How confident am I that this person embezzled money?" If you believe it around 73% confidence, ask yourself, "What would make it a 70?" and "What would make it a 75?" Then look for evidence in both directions.

Here is an interesting takeaway for you: *we cannot "prove" anything*. If someone ever says something is scientifically proven, they're misusing the word "proven." Science doesn't prove anything. It can't. Science can only demonstrate things. We find evidence that is consistent with gravity, medications, natural selection, and so on, but we might be wrong. If we disprove those things tomorrow, so be it. There are no factual hills to die on. We will infer facts as true until something better comes along, and then change hills. So, the best information we have today is just information that has not yet been disproven. We aren't right, we're less wrong.

When we're talking about things that we know, it's impossible to speak with absolute certainty. When we say we "know" something, we really mean that we infer something with a great degree of confidence. Evidence is vital in shaping our inferences. So, how do we know what kind of evidence can we trust?

Falsifiability: What kind of evidence can we use?

Since we are so reliant on evidence to narrow our range of possibilities, we want to make sure we're using good evidence because not all "evidence" is the same. Not all claims of fact are equally useful. Some claims of fact just can't be used to make inferences. For example, take this fun little thought experiment that was proposed by the cosmologist, Carl Sagan.[50] If I told you that next to you was a dragon, how would you respond? Most would request proof. So, I say that it's an invisible dragon, thus explaining why you can't see it. Do you believe me? Most would say no, but it still could be possible, couldn't it?

We're keeping our minds open, so you ask me to have the dragon make a noise. I counter that it's a silent dragon. It stays invisible so it can't be seen, stays quiet so it can't be heard. Staying silent helped it survive all those pesky dragon-slaying knights in the Middle Ages. If you haven't done it yet, you might start rolling your eyes, but you really want this dragon to be real, so you ask it to move something. Oops. I forgot to tell you, the dragon changes its density, so it passes through solid objects.

We admit the possibility there could be an invisible, soundless, massless dragon in the room. There's a non-zero chance, a chance above zero, even if it's really, really small. The chances could be 0.00000 with 3,000 zeros after the decimal, then a 1, but it's not zero. Although at a certain point, we have to ask the million-dollar question: what is the difference between an invisible, soundless, massless dragon and no dragon at all?

The claim that there's a dragon next to you becomes effectively the same as there being no dragon if we have no way of testing the presence of the dragon. A fact that cannot be verified is as useful as no fact.

Any claim that cannot be disproved is called unfalsifiable.[51] There is no way to disprove it, which means there's no way to use it.

Unfalsifiable claims aren't limited to the realm of thought experiments. They show up in the real world all the time. A family friend tells you that coconut oil will reverse your elderly relative's dementia. You give your relative coconut oil, and nothing changes. "You must have given it at the wrong time of day," the friend explains. You change the time of day, nothing changes. "Oh, it definitely works," responds the friend, "You must not have given it with food." You administer the oil with food, and nothing changes. If your friend insists the coconut oil works but you see no changes, then the coconut cure is unfalsifiable. Using the coconut oil is just as useful as not using it.

An old acquaintance on social media posts that the outcome of an election they didn't like was rigged. When a commenter says there is no evidence of fraud, the poster doubles down, "Of course there's no evidence, that's how you know it's a cover up!" The claim is unfalsifiable. The coconut oil might work, the election may have been rigged—but an unfalsifiable claim is as useful as no claim.

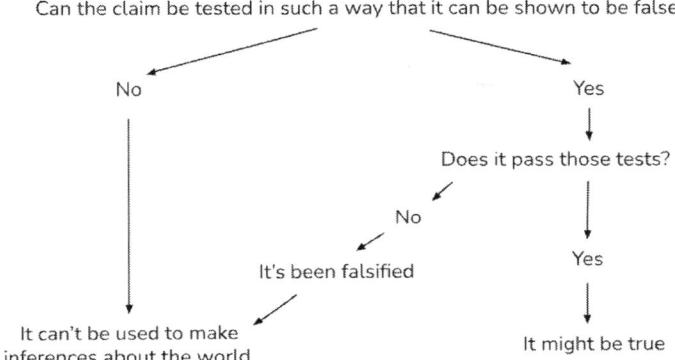

So, might a claim of fact be true? We don't "know" for sure, but we can become more confident. If the claim of fact keeps passing tests, then it really, really, really might be true but not absolutely true. Remember, we don't know things with absolute certainty. Even things we take for granted, like gravity (thankfully, gravity is falsifiable). If you let go of a pen and if it fell up, you would have just falsified gravity. If you found a modern-day cow skeleton that dates back to the Cretaceous period, then you would have falsified the theory of natural selection and we would have to rethink everything that we know about evolution. So, we treat facts like they are true even though tomorrow could be proven wrong. We work with the best information that we have.

The Burden of Proof: Where do we get evidence?

To know what's true, we make inferences. To make good inferences, we need evidence. To have good evidence, it must be falsifiable (i.e., testable). Where does this evidence come from? That brings us to **The Burden of Proof.** The British philosopher Bertrand Russell[52] posed the thought experiment that somewhere out in space between Mars and Jupiter there is a little teapot (thankfully, this is a falsifiable teapot as it's visible and has mass and blah, blah, blah—it's not like our dragon).

Let's pretend that you're having a hard time finding the tea pot. You can't definitively say it's *not* there because space is big, objects move in orbit, and the teapot could have moved to a spot where you just looked.

What Russell has done is sent you on a little errand to try to prove a negative. To prove a negative is to prove that something isn't there, which can't be done. None of us can prove that Bertrand Russell's teapot *is not* out there somewhere in space. In the same way, if I say there is a purple mouse in your room, you can't prove that there is no purple mouse somewhere in your room. That doesn't mean you should believe there's a purple mouse running around in your room. I made the claim, so I need to provide the evidence. I would need to fulfill the burden of proof.

The burden of proof is all about where evidence comes from. Evidence must come from the ones making the claim. If I say that there is a purple mouse running around in your room, how did I get to that conclusion? Even if I come to you with bad evidence, at least we'll have some evidence to start the conversation regarding what's true or not. Maybe I come to you with a little purple hair. It might've come from something else like a stuffed animal, towel, or fuzzy purple shirt. But at least now there is some evidence to start the discussion.

This feels intuitive at a certain level, but it's important to discuss because this is where many discussions break down in public discourse, especially when we get to things like conspiracy theories. If you ever want to start a conspiracy theory, you could weaponize the burden of proof. Please use your knowledge for good, but one of the things that conspiracies do is to shift the burden of proof to make other people prove a negative, which can't be done, which conspiracy theorists take as evidence they're right. "You can't find the soundstage where the government faked the moon landing? See! That's how good they are at cover-ups!"

That's what's so dangerous about the burden of proof. It is easy to shift the burden of proof onto someone else to prove you wrong. But we can only disprove claims once we have evidence, even if it's bad evidence like a little purple hair. In our debates, especially when it comes to issues of fact, we need to make sure that the burden of proof rests with those making the claim. To make a claim, we must provide evidence which starts the debate about what the evidence is telling us.

Even if we have fulfilled the burden of proof, and we have evidence that's testable, evidence doesn't necessarily speak for itself. Facts don't just tell their entire story. Finding a bunch of bones in the ground doesn't tell us life evolved through natural selection. It could just as well have been aliens playing a prank on us by hiding bones. So how do we explain the evidence that we have?

Occam's Razor: How do we explain our evidence?

Facts don't speak for themselves. They don't tell their stories, so how do we come up with explanations for our facts? How can we explain the presence of the purple hair in your room? How do we explain the existence of the fossils in the ground and other scientific facts? One way is by looking at it from William of Occam's point of view.

William of Occam was a friar from the 14th century who came up with a good way of approaching the problem of competing explanations for facts. For example, let's assume there is purple hair discovered in your room. My explanation is that there is a purple mouse running around your room. Someone else's explanation is that the hair came from a purple stuffed animal in the room. It has hairs that look exactly like the one we just found, *and* the stuffed animal has shed purple hairs like this one before.

We now have two explanations. My explanation that the hair came from a purple mouse could be true. There's a non-zero chance the hair came from a purple mouse even though we've never seen a purple mouse in the history of time before. Even if that chance is very, very small, it's still not zero. However, the chances it came from the purple stuffed animal seems more likely. Occam's Razor is a method to cut away one of the two explanations. How do we choose which one goes?

Occam's Razor suggests that "Entities should not be multiplied beyond necessity." "Entities" refers to explanations for evidence we have in front of us. That is, the simplest explanation is often the best explanation.

Even though it is perfectly possible the purple hair came from a purple mouse or from your stuffed animal, the most plausible and simplest explanation is that it came from the stuffed animal next to you as opposed to a purple mouse that has never been seen in nature, let alone in your room.

Occam's Razor doesn't guarantee we're going to end up with the correct explanation every time; we always must be open to being wrong. This purple hair might have come from a stuffed animal. It might have come from a mouse. If we must decide right now, how are we going to explain it? We'll go with the simplest explanation and be willing to change our minds if better evidence appears later.

So, where are we?

If we use the simplest explanation to connect our facts, *if* our facts fulfill the burden of proof, and *if* our facts are testable, *then* we can use them to make confident inferences that *might* just be the truth. *But...*

Even if a fact is true, it can still be misleading.

The CRAAP Test: How can you fact-check in your own life?

Suppose I develop a new pill I am going to call Speechacil. It is designed to treat headaches. In my testing of the drug, I find some useful results I can present to the public. If I'm going to sell my Speechacil pill, I can't use any false advertising, so I can't lie. I can only say things that are true. You find an advertisement from me that says, "No medicine alleviates headaches faster than Speechacil." Great. Let's assume for the sake of argument this is true. I ran a test wherein I gave the Speechacil pills to one group of people with headaches, I gave Tylenol to another group of people with headaches, I gave Advil to another group, and so on.

What if *all* their headaches disappeared after 15 minutes? Even though every group all got different pills, all their headaches went away after 15 minutes. Is my advertisement that no medicine cures headaches faster than Speechacil true?

Yes, it is true. Even if the pills all performed at the exact *same* rate, I can now honestly say that no other pill was *faster* than Speechacil. The thing is that when most of us read the sentence "No medicine alleviates headaches faster than Speechacil," we don't read that the medicines all performed at the same rate. We assume that Speechacil was the fastest and, therefore, the best. But that's not what the sentence says. The sentence says none of the other ones were faster. I don't have to make a pill that's better than anybody else's. I just have to make one that's about the same as everybody else's. I can write my ad honestly. What I've presented you is a fact. But *even true facts can be misleading*.

The **CRAAP Test** helps us navigate through true but misleading facts.[53] It is a series of filters you can use for actual information in your own life. You can also use it if you're preparing evidence for a report you're writing, if you're trying to make an informed decision about an election, or deciding which product to buy.

The CRAAP Test allows you to vet your information in a few different ways. When you come across a fact, whether it's a story in the news, hearsay on social media, or an academic study, ask yourself about its **Currency**. That is, is this information recent enough to be useful? Some topics have information that's changing all the time. On the other hand, some things don't, so you have to think about what's going to be the most useful for your circumstances. If I'm reading some kind of a study about the psychology of dating, I want to look at the date because many older studies only looked at heterosexual couples and didn't account for meeting online. If my study is about something like physics, and I read that Earth's gravity accelerates mass at 9.98 meters per second per second, then it might not matter if the information is old because the acceleration of gravity hasn't changed much in four billion years or so.

Once you've run a claim through a currency test, you can look at the next filter, **Relevancy**. Ask yourself how relevant this information is to what you are interested in. Different information is going to be presented for different audiences. If I'm reading information about retirement savings, and I found that information in AARP, an organization for a retired, older audience, that's going to have very different information than investment advice for college students. That's fine. Different people need different things, which is why it's so imperative to ensure you understand the target audience for the fact you're evaluating so you can properly gauge its relevance to you.

Next is **Authority**, which evaluates how qualified the author or source of the information is. If someone claims they are a doctor, do they have a Ph.D. from an accredited college or is it from an online degree mill? If they have a college issued doctorate, is it in the field of their expertise? A doctor with a Ph.D. in theatre is not as qualified to give health advice as a doctor of epidemiology. We also have to watch out for bias. Does this person have a dog in the fight? Does this person have an agenda? If I'm posting lots of information that might be related to politics, but I'm only getting my stories from Fox News, it's going to be very conservative. If I'm only getting my stories from MSNBC, that's going to be very liberally slanted.

The next A stands for **Accuracy**. This is especially important to leverage in the 21st century, living in the age of Google. Accuracy means verifying the information elsewhere, seeing if it has been reviewed by anybody else. We're especially looking for sources that can disprove the information we're vetting (remember confirmation bias from Chapter 2 and falsifiability from earlier?). If something survives being falsified, that's probably pretty good information. Have people tried to test this claim, tried to falsify it, and haven't been able to? Can we verify this information from a different source? If I find something in Fox News, it doesn't mean it's necessarily useless just because it's Fox. What if I can verify that same exact headline at MSNBC or from the Associated Press or from Reuters or from The Economist or BBC out in the UK? If we can verify information from other sources, then we can become a bit more confident in that information.

Finally, we're evaluating **Purpose**, my personal favorite. We need to ask ourselves *why* this information is being presented. Information is presented with different kinds of motivation. Often, information is presented to you so your attention can be sold to advertisers. Cable news didn't used to run twenty-four hours a day, seven days a week. It used to be that news was only on at 6:00 PM for about half an hour. That's it. Then the news cycle was born, and cable stations had to keep viewers hooked in order to sell advertising space. Cable news has to keep coming up with things that sound exciting and important to keep viewers listening. As they say, "If it bleeds, it leads."

Other questions we can ask about purpose is whether it's there to keep my attention, to inform, or maybe even for entertainment? Am I watching something that's actually a parody, and I'm supposed to be laughing as opposed to getting smarter? Maybe the information is designed to provoke. You see this a lot on social media. With social media, everyone is in charge of whatever they choose to share, and many people will share things out of a knee jerk response of being angry. Clickbait is born, and information we come across is designed to rile us up and get us mad.

For this purpose, always ask, "Who stands to gain from this information?" If I'm reading a headline that makes a Republican candidate look bad, maybe that's so the Democratic candidate looks good. I should be skeptical if I'm only seeing this information from democratic sources.

Take a step back from the information that you see. Interrogate its relevance, its intended audience. Look for biases. Try to verify the information elsewhere. Keep in mind who might benefit from the information being shared.

We can never be completely certain of anything; we infer our knowledge. With more evidence we can become more confident in the inferences we make. Even though we never get to absolute certainty, we can approach certainty. As for the kind of evidence that's useful for making inferences—if it can't be falsified, it's not useful. We need evidence that can be tested (because an invisible, weightless dragon might be the same thing as no dragon at all). As for where that evidence comes from, we can't start discussing issues of truth without any evidence because we can't prove a negative. To fulfill the burden of proof, people making claims need to have evidence for the claim. That which can be asserted without evidence can be dismissed just as easily. Once we have a collection of facts, we need to explain those facts. How do we explain them? William of Occam provides his razor, with which we can cut away redundant explanations. Usually, the simplest explanation is the best. And finally, there is the CRAAP Test, which will help you analyze information for any misleading facts.

These ideas can help you navigate disputes of fact. Since we won't reach complete certainty of facts, we're not really setting out to be right, we're trying to be *less wrong*. But "wrong" is a funny word, isn't it? On the one hand it means being factually incorrect (e.g., that answer is wrong), on the other it means being immoral (e.g., what the burglar did was wrong). Even if we can be less wrong, factually, how can we be less wrong, morally?

10 Tips on Issues of Fact

1. Score your confidence in facts

How confident are you that a given fact is true? Score your confidence from 0 (definitely false) to 100 (definitely true). Think about what would adjust your score up or down. We can't know things with absolute certainty, the best we can do is infer. So before claiming 100% certainty, always leave at least .01% open to other possibilities.

2. Stay open to any possibility

Assume that whatever we currently believe is wrong but is likely the *least* wrong. It hasn't been disproven yet. If something more convincing comes along, we'll accept that. Then *that* will be the least wrong thing we believe. On and on it goes, thanks to falsifiability.

3. Don't say something has been "proven"

Proof exists in math, not science. We cannot definitively prove anything. The best we can do is fail to *dis*prove something over and over again, but we can never prove something. The things we keep failing to disprove are the things we call "facts."

4. Be skeptical when someone says something is "proven"

If anyone tells you something is "scientifically proven," they either had an honest slip of the tongue, are trying to sell you something, or don't know what they are talking about. The latter two more are more common.

5. Don't believe a claim that can't be tested

A dragon that's invisible, weightless, and soundless may as well be no dragon at all. A fact that's impossible to test may as well be no fact at all.

6. If you make a claim, provide evidence

The burden of proof falls on those who make the claim to provide testable evidence.

7. Don't fall for the trap of trying to prove a negative

If someone challenges you to prove something is not there, that can't be done. You can't prove a negative. Once they provide you with evidence, then the conversation can move forward.

8. Think of rival explanations for the facts, especially if you don't like them

Facts don't tell complete stories by themselves. The stories we think of first might just be the stories we *want* to be true. Like Richard Feynman said, "The first principle is that you must not fool yourself—and you are the easiest person to fool."

9. Keep it simple

Use Occam's Razor to cut out redundant, unnecessary explanations. Often, the simplest explanation is the best.

10. Ask yourself, "Why is this information being presented to me?"

Use the CRAAP Test to examine the information's Currency, Relevance, Authority, Accuracy, and Purpose.

Chapter 7

Talk About What's Good

"No man chooses evil because it is evil; he just mistakes it for happiness, the good he seeks."

— Mary Wollstonecraft

"Conscience" is a word you've seen before. That little Jiminy Cricket-esque figure on our shoulder, whispering what's good and what's bad, so we can make good decisions. Conscience has a couple of key components, *con* and *science*. "Science" isn't just a subject you take in school. Science is a Greek word that literally means knowledge.[54] When you took a "science" class in school, you were really taking a "knowledge" class about issues of fact.

Then there's the prefix *con*, which comes from Latin. You'll recognize this from Romance languages like Italian or Spanish. *Con* means "with," and so to have a conscience is literally to act *with knowledge*. The word "conscience" reveals that *to be moral is to be informed*. We must have our facts straight before we can start making good, moral, ethical decisions.

We've been talking about different kinds of principles and tools you can use to discern fact from fiction, but what about issues of value? What are the principles we use to discern right from wrong? Admittedly, we're not going to be able to resolve the question here. Philosophy and religion have been exploring morality and ethics for centuries. But we can cover a few vital ideas that have massive influence over disagreements of value.

There are common lines of thinking and ethical principles that will show up in just about any kind of disagreement. As before, we'll start with the philosophical and move to more concrete applications. All these principles will be useful and can help you construct your own arguments or navigate with skepticism as you enter disagreements on issues of rightness and wrongness.

Because we are discussing right and wrong, we will be utilizing thought experiments designed to make you a little uncomfortable. You will need to make some decisions. Your decisions in these thought experiments will not be a reflection on your character. They won't make you a good person or a bad person. There is no shame, no blame. They are just for the sake of the thought experiments.

Utilitarianism

Let's imagine that you are the conductor of a train. *Chugga, chugga, chugga woo, woo!* (Or however many "chug-gas" are appropriate for each "woo woo." I'm not sure. You would know—you're the conductor.) You're going about your train-chugging day when you realize there are five people on the track ahead of you (Track A). These five people are going to die because they're standing right on the track. You try to brake, but your brakes aren't working. For some reason, they don't see the train. You yell and scream, and you pull the string to blow the train whistle, but they don't move. They can't hear you.

You're relieved when you see that there's an upcoming track you can change to (Track B). If you pull a lever, you will change tracks and you'll save the lives of the five people from Track A. Wonderful. But as you are about to pull the lever, you realize there's *one* person on Track B. If you change to Track B, that one person is going to die. Not from old age, not in a bed surrounded by their loved ones, but because your train will hit them. This person also cannot hear your approach.

I am going to ask you two questions. Remember, your answer is not a reflection of your character. It doesn't make you a good person or a bad person. There's no shame, no blame. It's just for the sake of the thought experiment. First, I'm going to ask what you think the right thing is for a person to do. Then I'm going to ask what you would do. Sometimes what we do isn't always what we think is the right thing to do. Maybe your two responses will be the same. Maybe you would choose to do something different than what you think is the morally right thing. Maybe you will do what you believe is the right thing, or maybe you won't. No problem.

Remember, if you pull the lever, the train changes to Track B and kills one person and saves five people.

Question one: Should a person pull the lever? Yes, or no?
Question two: Would *you* pull the lever? Yes, or no?

If you're the one forced to make the choice, it feels slightly more uncomfortable. Many will likely respond that pulling the lever is the right thing to do, and when asked what you, specifically, would do, many agree they would follow suit, even if there is resistance or reluctance. It's uncomfortable. Even though one person dies, we're saving five people and that's the right thing to do. If this has in any way resonated with your reasoning and the way you felt with this thought experiment, then you might be thinking like a utilitarian.

This is the first big approach in trying to articulate what makes something good or bad. **Utilitarianism** is the philosophical argument that what makes something good, right, moral, or ethical is what maximizes happiness for the greatest number or minimizes suffering for the greatest number.[55] We want to save the most lives. We want to reduce the number of deaths. We want to create happiness. We want to reduce anger and sadness, stuff like that. That's a very utilitarian approach to issues of value.

The Wrath of Khan embodies this sentiment when Spock says, "The needs of the many outweigh the needs of the few."[56] That's a very utilitarian thing to say in a moment of self-sacrifice. So, utilitarians say that the morality of a choice depends on the utility of the choice's outcomes—we're done, right? We've figured out morality! Well, not so fast.

Deontology

To get a more robust perspective on issues of value, we need to look at a competing philosophy of rightness and wrongness, which is **deontology**. Deontology, in some ways, is a direct response to utilitarianism. For this thought experiment, I'm going to have you imagine that you are a doctor.

You're all by yourself in the emergency room during the night shift. Nobody else, just you. At some point, a person stumbles through the front door and collapses on the ground unconscious. You check for a pulse, you check breathing, and everything seems normal. You run some more tests, and they all come back fine.

You are a very skilled doctor, but you don't know what brought them to you that night. This person can sleep through the rest of the night and wake up in the morning perfectly healthy to go about their business. Nice. Easiest patient ever! Except, this isn't your only patient. Asleep in the next room, you have five people who are going to die due to things that could be easily fixed with the right resources. One person is healthy, except for their heart. They need a new one. Another patient needs a new liver. Another patient, new lungs, and so on and so forth. Each of the five people needs one specific part to be whole, and if they don't get that part by tonight, they will die. But great news! Remember your mystery patient who stumbled in through the door? The tests you ran on your mystery patient showed that their organs would be a match for *all* five people.

As before, I am going to ask you two questions. Remember, your response is not a reflection of your character. It doesn't make you a good person or a bad person. No shame, no blame. It's just for the sake of the thought experiment.

Question one: Should a person harvest one patient to save the five other patients?
Question two: Would *you* harvest the one patient to save the five other patients?

It's likely most would say that we shouldn't harvest the organs of one person to save five. That makes sense. After all, that's murder. What would you do? While a utilitarian might declare Spock's noble, utilitarian catchphrase "the needs of the many outweigh the needs of the few," a deontologist might hear the same phrase in Niccolò Machiavelli's voice, translated to "the ends justify the means."[57] For a moral system based on deontology, rightness and wrongness are not based on outcomes.

Deontology says that adhering to certain rules or principles is what's moral. Rules like don't kill, don't steal, or don't lie. These guidelines are intrinsically ethical to a deontologist. It seems like we all became deontologists in the hospital when we are looking at the unconscious person. We can sacrifice one person to save five, but our hand gets shaky, we put the scalpel down, and we say, "This is wrong."

If you were a utilitarian on the train (pulling the lever), and a deontologist in the hospital (putting down the scalpel), your reasoning might sound like this: "On the train track it's my job to save the most lives. It's not a comfortable decision, but I've got to do what saves people." As a doctor, "I don't have the *consent* of this one person for their organs. I don't have the right to harvest this one person to save the five people." The difference between the train and the hospital might be the consent of the one person we would kill to save five. But here's the really uncomfortable thing: the train tracks and the hospital are the same thought experiment. They *feel* different because we dress them up with different language and different circumstances, but essentially all I did was ask the same question two times: *is it okay to sacrifice one person to save five?*

One of them is dressed up with train tracks. The other one is dressed up with hospital beds. It's really the same thought experiment. Let's pause for a moment to extract two key takeaways that will deepen our understanding of disagreements. One, is that many disagreements come down to a clash between outcomes (utilitarianism) and principles (deontology). Another is that we will come to *different* conclusions about the *same* issue depending on how it is presented to us.

Practical vs. Principle

The **practical** versus the **principle** are two big philosophical approaches that drive much of the disagreement in our public discourse. Sometimes we argue because we want the best outcomes, sometimes we argue to defend certain principles. Once you know this, you can start to recognize the clash between the practical and principle as the undercurrent of many real-word controversies.

For example, the debate over gun laws is a perfect example of utilitarianism versus deontology. On the one hand, gun violence kills people. There is a body count. There are shootings in public spaces. The utilitarian in us argues that it's important to restrict guns to save lives. On the other hand, deontologically, we have constitutional rights like the right to keep and bear arms. It's the Second Amendment, just after freedom of speech and religion. That's very important. That's not just some afterthought. This creates a clash between safety (practical) and freedom (principle).

Another related example involves technology and privacy. Perhaps being able to break into the phone of a shooter can help save lives. After the tragic 2015 San Bernardino shooting, the FBI tried to access a locked iPhone belonging to a shooter by going directly to Apple, who refused to decrypt the phone.[58] On the one hand, access to that phone might be able to reveal the names of conspirators, and we could stop future shootings. Practical. On the other hand, if Apple can unlock one encrypted phone, they can unlock any encrypted phone, then there is no such thing as privacy. What kind of world are we trying to save if it's not one where we have any freedoms after we're done? Principle. These are not simple questions, and I can't pretend to solve them here, but I think it's probably helpful for us to be able to articulate the kinds of practical and principle-based concerns we encounter on either side of a debate. What outcomes are the utilitarian arguments looking for? What principles are the deontological arguments looking to preserve?

We will often develop tunnel-vision for the side we support and neglect the ethical approach someone else takes when they disagree. If I side with the FBI and argue for the interests of safety, I will likely try to "convince" someone who disagrees with me by speaking like a utilitarian. "Look how many people were hurt," "Here's how many lives we could save," but if their position is one rooted in principle, I need to speak to the interests of preserving the right to privacy. "No one has the right to access your private data—absolutely. Our right to privacy should be defended at all costs. But how do we exercise our rights if we're dead?"

Identifying the practical or principle-based undercurrent behind real-world debates is essential because it allows us to start speaking each other's moral languages. Using practical arguments to persuade someone thinking in principle-based terms is like speaking Spanish to a Martian. If we are going to speak to each other productively about disputes, we need to speak the same moral language.

So, that's it, right? We've fixed public discourse? Just tell everyone about utilitarianism and deontology, practical versus principle, speak the same blah blah blah? Well, not exactly. Identifying the undercurrents of each other's ideas is an excellent start, but before we can successfully navigate issues of value, we need to identify a significant obstacle within *ourselves*.

Polarization

Identifying the clash between the practical and principle is vital for discussions of what's right and wrong. But as you navigate disagreements of value, you should be aware of the biggest villain in your way: polarization.

Here's a conversation prompt I've used with classes and friends that works better than it should: pick any two unusual items around you and ask, "Which one of these would win in a fight?" Suppose you pick up a water bottle and a pen. People don't need more than a few seconds to make their decision and start generating arguments.

Team Water Bottle will come up with arguments like:
- The bottle is bigger and heavier, it can crush the pen
- The bottle is dense and impervious to any damage from a little plastic pen
- Water is a life-giving, elemental force—a pen is just a cheap piece of plastic

Team Pen will come up with arguments like:
- The pen is sharp and can stab the water bottle
- The pen is smaller and more agile
- The pen can write an insulting note and hurt the bottle's feelings

People start off by tossing out general ideas and participatory nods, but eventually an idea lingers on their mind longer than the others, and they engage with it. "Hold on, an insulting note? If the bottle can be insulted, then the pen can be insulted by the bottle splashing it. That's *worse* because the pen will get hurt feelings *and* the ink dilutes!" They dig in their heels and defend their position.

After the back and forth—even getting pulled in myself sometimes—it's always sobering to remember that the question is ridiculous. Which one would win in a fight? A pen and a bottle can't fight. There is no answer to the question. But a nonsensical premise doesn't stop people from getting competitive.

Our Stone Age ancestors were used to traveling in small groups, defending the ingroup from rival outgroups. We still have those same tribal tendencies—and where tribes don't exist, we will *invent* them. Cat people versus dog people. iPhone users versus Android users. Red Sox fans versus Yankees fans. Marvel versus DC. Sales department versus HR. We are very good at creating and joining tribes.

Polarization is always looming whenever we enter any public discourse that divides opinions. With that in mind, here's another little thought experiment for you.

There are two people: one is named A and the other is named B. The person called B is going to die, but thanks to the magic of science, we have invented a funny-looking helmet.

The helmet doesn't really go with very many outfits. It's big, cumbersome, and awkward. It's the size of a couple basketballs. It connects to an identical helmet worn by A. As long as A wears this helmet and stays connected to the identical helmet worn by B, then B is going to be just fine. This doesn't really harm A. It doesn't cause any undue distress, and it doesn't make A any weaker, necessarily. They can both still go on about their lives, but they must wear the helmets twenty-four hours a day, seven days a week, and they have to stay close to each other for the wire that connects the helmets. The length of the wire isn't very long, so A and B are always with each other whenever they sleep, whenever they eat, and even whenever they go out on dates with their significant others (if they can get a significant other in this new lifestyle). The good news is that as long as both A and B wear these helmets for one year, then they can both take off the helmets and go about their lives. Yay! But if either A or B takes off the helmet even for a second before that year is up, B will die.

Let's imagine these two people are strangers. They don't know each other. What should A do? What do you think A has the right to do? One year is a long time, and it may be taxing on A. Maybe A wants to have a dating life or is tired of sharing the shower all the time. It's possible A might start having second thoughts over the course of the year. So, the question that I put to you, if you had to choose "yes" or "no," is the following:

Does A have the right to take off the helmet?

When I pose this question to groups and classes, I find the vast majority will say yes, A does have the right. It doesn't mean they are looking to kill B (or that you are in case you had the same answer). Let's lay on some pressure to make this thought experiment as uncomfortable as possible.

Instead of strangers, A and B are best friends. They've grown up on the same street. They've been with each other through thick and thin, through the good times and the bad. I'm going to ask you again: Does A have the right to take off the helmet?

What I tend to find is that there's more hesitation, but, ultimately, the majority of my audiences will say yes, A still has the right. If you're still saying yes, even if it's a bit more difficult or begrudging, we're going to kick the scenario up another notch.

A and B are siblings, *and* they are best friends. Does A have the right to take off the helmet?

This is where I tend to see about five to ten percent who had been saying "yes" switch to "no." A no longer has the right. Now, if you are still holding out and having an easy time saying yes, let's kick it up another notch.

A and B are strangers again, but what if B is ten years old? Just a kid. Does A have the right to take off the helmet?

I'll tend to see more resistance here when I pose this variation to groups. People have a hard time saying yes, or at least saying yes so quickly, but I often still have more than half of people trend toward saying yes, A has the right. Fair enough. If that's you, let's lay on the pressure even more.

What if B is *one* year old? It's the day of B's first birthday party with the clowns and the balloons and the magicians. Does A have the right to take off the helmet?

This scenario causes yet more strain. But if you still say yes, A does have the right to take off the helmet; then what if B is *one day* old? It is B's *literal* birthday. Even though it's B's literal birthday, does A have the right to take off the helmet?

This is where the real heavy resistance starts for people who have been saying "yes" all the way through; they start to flip to "no." And the people who are still saying yes are doing so very reluctantly.

This thought experiment is not like the train tracks or the hospital scenario, which are purely hypotheticals existing in an ethical vacuum for your consideration. You may have already picked up that this thought experiment is about a very real ethical dilemma our society faces: *abortion*. Does one person's right to their body outweigh another person's right to live?[59]

Abortion may be the best example of polarization in public discourse. On one side, there are those who self-identify as pro-life and say that abortions should not be allowed. On the other, there are those who identify as pro-choice and say that abortion should be allowed. The pro-life group calls the pro-choice group "baby killers" and the pro-choice group calls the pro-life group "woman-haters."

I'm not sure what your personal stance is. This book isn't designed to convince you either way. But I bring it up here because the issue of abortion can teach us a lot about the nature of our disagreements. This first half of the thought experiment is designed to make my pro-life readers somewhat uncomfortable. Why? Because when I pose the dilemma of A's and B's helmets, I frequently find that those who identify as pro-life say, "Yes, A can remove the helmet." In fact, they'll even say yes, several times, even if B is a kid or a one-year-old or a newborn baby.

This is ethically incompatible with opposing abortion, but when it comes to the real-world issue of abortion, they will say no abortions. The idea that a person can end the life of another if they're cordoning off boundaries to their own bodies is not *similar* to the issue of abortion—it *is* the issue. Let's hang on to this thought and move into the second half of the thought experiment. This second half is designed to make the pro-choice readers uncomfortable.

There are three trimesters of pregnancy, each one lasting three months. If you are pro-choice, I'd like you to think about when it's okay to have the abortion. Is it the first trimester? When I pose this question in discussion, many who identify as pro-choice will say it's permissible in the first trimester. How about in the second trimester? Many of them still agree, but maybe with a moment to think. How about the third trimester? Some start to hesitate here and are not quite sure. For those who say the third trimester is okay, I start to push the envelope. What about one week before the delivery date? I lose many pro-choice supporters one week out from the due date. If that's the case, fair enough. But if you are okay with one week before the due date, how about the *day* before the due date? If you are still okay with that, how about the day of delivery? Or just a moment after birth?

It's rare, but occasionally, in a class discussion, I've gotten students to say yes all the way through to just after birth. Can we abort then? If I happen to get someone that says yes all the way through, they have usually become accustomed to delivering a string of yeses to my questions, and it's always a quizzical moment of self-awareness to realize there already exists a word for killing a baby: murder. In that moment of self-awareness comes the position shift: oh no, you can't do that. That's obviously, clearly murder. Well, how come? What's the intrinsic difference between a baby out of the womb and a baby inside the womb?

What's the difference between time x versus time y? This question is still relevant for anyone who is pro-choice irrespective of when during the pregnancy timeline you decided abortion is no longer permissible. If you said that an abortion is okay in the first trimester but not the second, that's only a difference of a second. In every pregnancy, there exists a date on the calendar marking the end of the first trimester at 11:59 pm. Once 61 seconds elapses, it becomes 12:00 am of the second trimester, and now the baby cannot be aborted. Why? What changed in that sixty-first second?

Perhaps the inflection point has to do with the survivability of the baby. For example, once a fetus develops a heartbeat we shouldn't abort it, so the heartbeat becomes the standard for the right to life. But does that mean people without a heartbeat lose the right to life? If a person's heart stops beating, we administer CPR or we use a defibrillator. Perhaps a baby can no longer be aborted once it's able to breathe? After all, a breathing baby is able to survive outside of the mother. But if breathing becomes the standard for a right to life, does a person lose that right if they are unable to breathe? Again, CPR tries to resuscitate those who aren't breathing, and we have ventilators to assist those whose lungs aren't up to the task. So, biological markers like heartbeats and breathing don't seem to be a good way to distinguish when it's permissible to abort.

When does a fetus become a baby? When is it okay to abort versus when is it not okay to abort? Whether our answer is based on a timeline or on biological development, it seems that our line in the sand is going to have to be arbitrary. Whatever standard we settle upon will not be an objective reflection of a fetus's "babyhood," it will be to relieve our own discomfort. Even if you are pro-choice, the concession still must be made that abortion is killing.

This tacit concession is revealed by examining the language we use in practice. If someone has an abortion, they're aborting a *fetus*. But if someone has a miscarriage, they've lost the *baby*. Why is there a difference there? Because it absolves us from mental discomfort. This section of the book has been designed to return us to that discomfort. For pro-life readers, the discomfort is in conceding that the right to one's own body outweighs someone else's right to live. For pro-choice readers, the discomfort is in conceding that abortion is killing.

There is a name for this mental discomfort. It's called **cognitive dissonance**, and it might just save us all. Cognitive dissonance is the mental friction we experience whenever we hold two incompatible ideas. For example, a smoker who enjoys smoking but also wants to be a good role model to their kids will experience cognitive dissonance. When we experience this discomfort, we usually pick one. One idea must give way to the other one (we pick enjoyment and keep smoking or we pick being a role model and stop smoking). Our primary objective becomes getting out of the discomfort. Alternatively, many of us will rationalize the incompatibility away to resolve the discomfort (e.g., choose smoking *and* role model by teaching the kids to "do as I say, not as I do"—that works, right?). The point is, we don't like dissonance. We dislike it so much that we change our actions or rationalize our beliefs to make the dissonance go away. But as painful as cognitive dissonance is, it might be your greatest ally against the real villain of public discourse.

Remember the villain of public discourse? **Polarization** is our tendency to split our discourse into sharply contrasting positions. One of the reasons we do this is to avoid the mental discomfort that comes with moral greyness. If a pro-life person believes a person's right to their own body outweighs someone else's right to live, they believe a central tenet of pro-choice ideology. If someone pro-choice believes abortion is murder, then they believe a central tenet of pro-life ideology. The exercises we've conducted together imparts a vital realization to combat polarization: our opinions have more in common than we realize.

Ask a person what their stance is on abortion, and they can often tell you which side they're on. Ask them nuanced questions about the ethical dilemmas involved without mentioning abortion, and the sides become harder to distinguish. In fact, even changing the specific wording of identical questions yields different results. A Vox/PerryUndem survey found that nine percent more people agreed with the statement "Women should have a legal right to safe and accessible abortion in almost all cases" than the statement "Abortion should be legal in almost all cases."[60] The way we talk about issues is vitally important.

Abortion is among the most polarizing topics in public discourse, so it's surprising to see how much overlap there is in people's opinions. Our opinions have far more in common than we realize, but the way we talk about those opinions becomes extremely polarized.

It's our *discourse* that gets split into different camps, but not necessarily *us* who get split into different camps.

If we agree more than we realize, we need to work on how we talk about those opinions. We can start by realizing we have "conditions"—not sharply contrasted positions. We have conditions under which we would change our minds. If I am someone who identifies as pro-life, there are conditions under which I would agree that a person can have an abortion. If I identify as pro-choice, there are conditions under which I would agree that abortion is killing, and we shouldn't do it. The real question becomes finding out what those conditions are. This is the secret question we can ask ourselves to beat polarization and use to reveal common ground we have with people who deeply disagree with us:

Under what conditions would I change my mind?

If I oppose abortion, under what conditions would I change my mind? Maybe I would change my mind if the pregnancy is endangering the life of the mother, which makes it a utilitarian solution. If I am pro-choice, under what conditions would I change my mind? Maybe if the mother's health could be completely protected during pregnancy and birth. As medical technology advances more and more, what if childbirth were painless and we could find every child a loving home, guaranteed? Maybe then there would be no need for abortions because we can look out for everyone.

In the gym, they say, "No pain, no gain." A sore bicep after a long day doing curls is uncomfortable, but it's a sign you're doing something right. Cognitive dissonance is the sore bicep of good discourse. It's uncomfortable, but it means you're truly considering opinions outside your own. It's difficult to feel cognitive dissonance, to enter that uncomfortable middle ground where we hold multiple conflicting ideas. But if we can get ourselves into that uncomfortable space, we pull away from the polarized edges, and we can start articulating the conditions under which we would change our minds. That is where the magic happens, that's where real public discourse about right and wrong can really start to take shape.

Moral Foundations Theory

Polarization is one of the big villains in our psychology that's more or less built into us. It's one of the things that we must work to overcome. What are some other things we already have hardwired into our own psychology?

If I take a pen from my right hand, and I put it in my left hand, would that make you mad? Is that a moral issue? Would that be "wrong" to do? Probably not. Most of us see that as an inert, amoral, neutral event. But if I said that everyone who likes dogs more than cats should pay more taxes, would you raise an eyebrow? Does that seem a bit "wrong"? That seems more like a moral issue.

Why are some issues just neutral, inert events, like changing a pen around, versus other issues being very anger-inducing? After all, what's anger-inducing for one person might be totally neutral to someone else, like eating certain kinds of foods or wearing certain kinds of clothes on certain days of the week and in certain colors and certain ways. Why are some things moral issues and other things not? A moral psychologist by the name of Jonathan Haidt and his colleagues were very interested in why certain things are moralized. What they found out was that across different cultures, we all tend to moralize certain things and not others. Haidt and his colleagues articulated what is now called **Moral Foundations Theory**.[61]

What Haidt discovered is we're all born with a kind of moral template. We have a certain recipe for which things ruffle our feathers and which things don't. We inherit this template, so even if we are taught which things are good and bad, we would still have a baseline instinct for morality, just to different degrees for each of these different moral foundations. If we can unpack what these different moral foundations are for ourselves and for others, then we can enter a very different kind of healthy disagreement with more precision. You'll also see that laws tend to stem directly from these moral foundations. You can learn about your moral foundations at www.YourMorals.org.

The first moral foundation that Haidt and his colleagues discovered was **harm**. We tend to moralize issues wherein someone is hurt. Of course, we have moral issues around killing. We know not to kill, hurt, or assault people. Harm could take other more nuanced forms, like psychological harm or emotional harm. Abuse isn't just physical. It could also be psychological and emotional, but we tend to moralize those issues because they still involve forms of harm.

The second moral foundation is **fairness.** We tend to care about issues wherein some people are treated differently than others, especially for what seem to be very arbitrary reasons. Generally speaking, we want equality. At least, as long as you have a high score on the foundation of fairness, then you care very much about equality.[62] If you had a low score for fairness, then issues of equality probably aren't that big a deal to you. For those of us with high scores, issues of fairness might include things like the equal treatment of women, those with disabilities, or the LGBTQ+ community. We also have laws, policies, and rules in place that stem from issues of fairness. For example, the civil rights movement, the Americans with Disabilities Act, or Title IX. Human resources offices exist to look out for issues of fairness, to make sure that everyone is generally treated equally to each other.

The third moral foundation is **ingroup loyalty**, which is whenever we're looking out for the wellbeing of our ingroup. Now, our ingroups could be small, like a group of friends or a family group. It could also be larger. Growing up in Hawai'i, we would always ask, "What school you go?" Our ingroup could be our alma mater or our communities. Some people will tattoo their zip codes on themselves, or maybe put their zip codes on their cars as stickers. Our ingroup could also be a country. Flying a flag is a display of one's solidarity with a national ingroup. We have all kinds of ingroups, and if we have a high score for ingroup loyalty, then we care very much about threats to our ingroups, especially threats from within, like if someone betrays the ingroup. An example might be a brother or sister who rats out their sibling, or someone who commits treason. The United States has passed laws regarding treason, and companies may have policies about corporate espionage. Both of these entities are looking out for their ingroup.

The next moral foundation is the foundation of **authority**. If we have a high score for authority, then we care very deeply about making sure we show respect for legitimate authorities, and we care very deeply if someone seems to undermine that authority. We have many rules regarding insubordination. It seems wrong for an employee to talk back to a boss, for a kid to sass their parents, and for a US citizen to burn the American flag. These all stem from our concern for authority.

The final moral foundation is **purity**. If you have a high score for purity, then you're concerned with how we elevate ourselves above our "disgusting" nature. We're trying to be better than our natural base, crass, or vulgar selves. An example of this is cursing. What even is a bad word? A word is just air you squeeze through your mouth. There's no such thing as bad noises or good noises, but the sense we have for bad words comes from a sense of purity. In the same way, some people view tattoos and piercings as treating the body in a vulgar way, leading to moralizing the treatment of our own body. It's interesting how different groups of people with high purity scores will have different issues.

For example, people who tend to identify as politically conservative will have purity concerns relating to sex and chastity, like no sex before marriage, sex is only between a man and a woman, or kinky sex is shameful. People who tend to identify as being politically liberal with high purity scores often care about food concerns, such as how food is harvested, whether it's organic or GMO, or avoiding processed foods.[63] As before, laws and regulations are created from concerns of purity, such as public decency laws.

The five moral foundations are harm, fairness, ingroup loyalty, authority, and purity. You may not have high scores for all of them. You might have some that are higher and some that are lower, but nonetheless, they're worth knowing because they're the moral foundations for people all around the world. Of course, our scores can change over time. As we learn things from our parents, attend Sunday schools, or become educated and have life experiences, our scores may go up and down.

If we know what the moral foundations are in our audience, then we know what kinds of arguments we might present. If we're in front of an audience that has a low score for authority, then having arguments about respecting legitimate authority won't be very persuasive. If we have an audience with high scores in fairness, then speaking to equality and looking out for mistreated groups can be very persuasive.

The Monkeysphere

Let's talk about monkeys for a moment. Did you know the size of a monkey's brain correlates to the size of its troop?[64] If a primatologist goes out into nature and measures the size of a monkey skull, they can predict how many other monkeys are going to be traveling within that group. This phenomenon has been nicknamed the Monkeysphere. The size of the brain only has room for so many people in a social group to keep track of, and that's how large the social group is. It scales up to primates like chimps and gorillas, and also...to humans.

Researchers have also measured the human brain to make a prediction about how large the Monkeysphere of a human ought to be. What they found with their correlation was that humans should have in their orbits around 150 people.

That's roughly the number of relationships we keep track of; individuals for whom we have empathy and compassion, whom we can reach out to and chat with, and wish them a happy birthday.

For a long time, this was quite speculative. We didn't really have a good way to measure this. It was a cool prediction that we could verify with other monkeys and primates, but we couldn't necessarily verify the phenomenon concretely with humans until social media. In recent years, as more and more people adopt social media platforms, we now have concrete, tangible ways to measure human interaction on a day-to-day basis. There are people with four thousand Facebook friends, but they're not keeping in touch with all of them. In that case researchers can measure the actual messages sent between users. Researchers discovered social media users tend to keep in actual contact with anywhere from 100 to 200 people.[65]

Keep the Monkeysphere in mind as we look at the interesting relationship between moral foundations and politics. Jonathan Haidt and his colleagues measured the moral foundations of people across different countries along how liberal or conservative they were. What they found was fascinating. Haidt and his colleagues noticed people who identify as being politically liberal would have very high scores for harm and fairness but low scores for ingroup loyalty, authority, and purity. So, to someone who identifies as liberal, it's a really big deal if someone gets punched (harm) or if a gay person couldn't get married (fairness). However, a liberal would not be particularly concerned if another person were leaking company secrets (loyalty), burning a flag (authority), or using recreational drugs (purity).

The data also suggest the more people rated themselves as conservative, the more all five moral foundations started to converge until they were all equally important. They even found some evidence that in extreme conservatism, harm and fairness received *lower* scores then loyalty, authority, and purity. That is, the scores of the moral foundations you would see in a liberal begin to flip for conservatives. So, for someone who's fairly conservative, a person being mistreated (fairness) would be just as big of a deal as burning a flag (authority). For someone who is very conservative, an issue of harm or fairness is not as important as an issue of purity, ingroup loyalty, or authority. So, someone burning a flag would be taken very seriously (authority), but someone not getting equal access to voting rights would not be as serious (fairness).

Haidt noticed this same trend in Europe, the Middle East, South America, and Asia. This suggests our tendency toward political leanings is at least in part driven biologically. What does this mean for us?

The big villain of our public discourse is polarization, our talks tend to split into sharply contrasting sides. No matter what side we're on, liberal or conservative, we consider ourselves the good guys and we must defeat the other side, the bad guys.

But imagine if your team won. Let's live in a hypothetical world for a second. If we identify as being liberal, what if tomorrow you won? Everyone, when you woke up tomorrow, was liberal. They would have high scores of harm and fairness and low scores of ingroup loyalty, authority, and purity. That's great, except different times in history create different problems which call for different kinds of solutions. There are always different problems, and we will need different approaches to solve them. If everyone in the world had high scores of fairness, that would be terrific because we would have the civil rights movement. We would have the Americans with Disabilities Act, and we could look out for issues of inequality, but we might have a harder time with issues of stability where we have to protect the ingroup from an outgroup. During certain times in history, like wartime, it's important to have a powerful sense of national patriotism to look out for the ingroup.

If we're conservative, and we woke up tomorrow and everyone was conservative, that would be great when we have to look out for the ingroup and defend against outgroups. It wouldn't necessarily be the best for those times in history when issues of progress are going to be most important, like social change; giving women the right to vote or starting the civil rights movement.

Having different people with different scores is a pretty good thing. If you're a liberal, it's a good thing that conservatives are around because they're looking out for your blind spots. If you're a conservative, it's a good thing liberals are around because they're also looking out for your blind spots.

In a way, that means that our job isn't beating the other team. We *need* each other with these different kinds of scores. We keep track of each other and help each other out because if we can improve the discourse, improve our dialogue, and distill the best solutions from all these different perspectives, then we can do anything.

What we can do is look at our own Monkeysphere. For many of us, our Monkeysphere is just our own family or friends, maybe community, state, or country. Everyone is "random." But what if our Monkeysphere was bigger? What if it accounted for everyone in the world?

The ancient Greeks had a word for this: *cosmopolitan*. Polis was the word for city, and cosmos, the universe. To be a cosmopolitan is to be a citizen of the cosmos. Every person is your fellow citizen, the entire world is your nation. If we could expand our Monkeysphere to the point where we can find others as members of our ingroup, we can start to improve the discourse because we know it's a good thing that they're around to disagree with us.

Penn Jillette, one half of the magician duo Penn and Teller, was interviewed in 2020 about politics, and he was not terribly fond of who had won the most recent US presidential election.[66] Jillette said he was trying out an experiment to stop referring to people as "them" and to refer only to "those of us." Even though it was difficult for him, he wanted to stop talking about the "people who voted for..." and instead talk about "*those of us* who voted for..." It was a difficult, painful thing to do for someone who wasn't happy about the political situation at the time, but he was trying to expand his Monkeysphere from the biological default of 150 to everyone, so he could contribute to a better public discourse. We can too.

10 Tips on Issues of Value

1. Spot the Practical-Principle tug-of-war hidden in the issue

Many controversies come down to a clash between practical concerns and principles. One common clash is safety versus freedom (e.g., gun control, vaccinations, online privacy). Pinpointing what is practical and what is principle allows you to see the real issue behind the issue.

2. Meet others where they are

Once you see the issue behind the issue, speak to the interest of the other person. If you argue for safety, and your partner argues for freedom, you will both speak past each other. Meet them on their deontological terms. How does your position advance freedom? And vice versa with utilitarian positions and arguments.

3. Notice your opinion "ingroups" and "outgroups"

Apple versus Android, Red Sox versus Yankees, Democrats versus Republicans, Marvel versus DC. If we don't have ingroup/outgroup divisions, we will invent them. Spot the idea groups you gravitate toward, whether they are significant or trivial issues.

4. Always be aware of what conditions would change your mind

There must be some conditions, otherwise, we're just creating more polarization.

5. Ask about what might change someone else's mind

Asking why a person believes what they do often helps them dig their heels in. Ask instead what would change their mind, even a little. "How certain are you, on a scale of 1 to 10? … A 9? Perfect. What do you think would move you to an 8?"

6. Consider yourself and the person you disagree with as being in the same "ingroup"

We tend to have more opinions in common with each other than we realize.

7. Know your moral foundations

Harm, fairness, loyalty, authority, and purity. You will prioritize certain moral foundations more than others. Those prioritizations will shape the way your disagreements with other people unfold.

8. Appreciate people with concerns for different moral foundations

Someone you disagree with probably prioritizes the moral foundations differently than you do, but you are not on different teams. They are looking out for your blind spots.

9. Expand your Monkeysphere

By default, you will keep track of about 150 people as "people" while everyone else becomes peripheral. Try to expand your Monkeysphere as best you can to include as many people as you can. On Earth, we are all part of the same ingroup. All we have is each other.

10. Say "those of us"

A practical way to expand your ingroup is to speak in terms of "us" and "we." It's not "People who voted for _____," it is "*Those of us* who voted for _____."

PART III: Public Speaking

Chapter 8

Prepare Exceptional Presentations

"Give me six hours to chop down a tree and I will spend the first four sharpening the axe."
— Abraham Lincoln

What are some easy-to-adopt skills that can be used by any speaker to dramatically improve the quality of their presentation? A presentation is only as successful as the quality of its preparation. Even what appears to be impressive impromptu speaking is only possible because the speaker has already given a lot of thought to their ideas or has spoken about their ideas in different contexts. Like the speaker Scott Berkun said, "All good public speaking comes from good private thinking."[67] Let's talk about how to prepare our ideas.

You can take your idea for a topic and start breaking it up into a few bite-sized chunks. When many of us think about a presentation, we see it as this big monolithic chunk of time that we must figure out how to fill. Instead, start viewing presentations more like little Lego bricks. They're composed of little individual parts that are easy to do one little block at a time. One part of the presentation might be one or two sentences, then another sentence or two, and now you have a killer presentation without feeling like you've exerted a ton of effort. You're just replicating things that effective speakers have done before you.

There is no right way to give a talk. If, for example, a year from now you are off presenting in the workplace, and you skip the "preview statement" (which we're going to discuss), no one in the audience is going to judge you for that. There's no way you're *supposed* to do it. In math, if you skip the order of operations, you get the wrong answer. But presentation skills are best practices—tools that tend to work well for most topics and for most speakers.

You pick and choose which skills you think are going to be the most effective. If you think something's not going to work, if you think now's not the time for a preview statement and you can articulate why, fair enough, it's your talk. You're the boss. But at least be aware of these tools so you can use them or ignore them intentionally. It's like Pablo Picasso said, "Learn the rules like a pro so you can break them like an artist." These are some of the rules you want to learn like a pro. Just remember this little phrase: "GREAT Points TOO."

GREAT Points TOO

This is your cheat sheet, your unfair advantage over your colleagues who feel frenzied and panicked when preparing a presentation. Here are the concepts each step stands for...

G: Get the audience's attention
R: Relate your topic to the audience
E: Explain your expertise
A: Aim for ONE big idea
T: Tell 'em what you're gonna tell 'em

Points: Deliver your points

T: Tell 'em what you told 'em
O: Offer a takeaway
O: Own your exit

If you freeze preparing for a presentation because you can't think of what to say, this little pocket-sized structure will be the secret Swiss Army knife for your voice.

GREAT

Get the audience's attention

Instead of starting off with a blank slate as the presenter, you jump in. It is not a big blank space of six minutes you need to fill, or whatever the time limit is. Instead, start with a strategy for your opening words. *Do not start by simply* stating your name and topic. Do not let your first word be "uh," "um," or "so." Grab their attention. This may feel like unhelpful advice, especially if you don't think of yourself as a creative or interesting person, but here are four different strategies you can use for the opening line. It does not matter what your topic is, but these strategies will help you in crafting an opening that will catch people's attention.

You can always fall back on a **quote**. No matter what your topic is, someone somewhere has said something interesting related to it. In the age of Google, you can find it. If you absolutely can't find the source of the quote, you can always use the old fallback of saying something along the lines of "it has been said" or "as you've probably heard." That said, it is always best to use a quote you can attribute.

Another strategy you can employ is the **unusual fact**. People love unusual facts. Avoid common knowledge because, if there's a high likelihood the audience knows it, it won't grab their attention. Please don't ever start a presentation by defining a word according to the dictionary. Find something surprising. Again, thanks to the age of Google and the Internet, it is quite easy to find unusual facts related to your topic. For example, not many people realize that Tyrannosaurus Rex lived closer to our time in history than to the time of the Stegosaurus.[68] Another fact: not many people realize the technology in their smartphone is more sophisticated than the technology that landed us on the moon.[69] These cool or interesting facts cause your audience to perk up and check in to your presentation.

We can also use a **story**. Stories are great because they are so versatile. We often think stories are just for kids. Nope.

PREPARE EXCEPTIONAL PRESENTATIONS   215

Adults love stories too. Adults are kids too, just taller. The movie industry makes billions of dollars because humans love stories.

Finally, you can use a **rhetorical question**, which is a question just there for effect or to provoke a thought. Don't ask a question that requires an audience response because you do not want to be the speaker that gives up the floor as soon as you begin. You want to use the floor to start strong. There's a place for audience interaction, but you were just given the floor—don't give it up with your first words. It's a presentation, not a town hall meeting. Also, please don't begin by asking the audience to close their eyes and imagine something. Everything that can be imagined with our eyes closed can be imagined with them open. It's too overdone, most audiences won't do it anyway, and most speakers forget to tell the audience to open their eyes again (betraying the audience's trust and making them defiantly keep their eyes open for the next speaker who tells them to close their eyes).

Those are four great ways to start a presentation, but they definitely are not the only ways. An attention grabber is crucial because the audience can think a lot faster than you can talk. They will be inclined to think about their own lives, what they want for lunch, what they're going to do when they get home, so this helps them switch the mental channel and tune into you. Once you have your audience listening, it's time for the single most important part of any introduction.

Relate your topic to the audience

What's in it for your audience? Once the audience tunes in, they want to know what's in it for them. Your next lines need to shift the attention back to them. If the presentation has no benefit for your audience, you are just making noise. How does your topic tie into their lives? What will they be able to see that used to be invisible? What will they appreciate that they used to take for granted? What will they be able to do that they weren't able to? You don't need to prove that your presentation is vital to their lives, that they should drop everything and rededicate their lives to the subject of your talk; but their lives should be improved in some small way.

Explain your expertise

Why are *you* the one talking about this? After you grab the audience's attention, after you demonstrate what's in it for them, it is time to tie yourself to the topic. You can demonstrate your expertise, your interest, or even how this may be affecting you or your group personally. What extra 10% experience, interest, or expertise do you have that your audience does not? Think about and share that extra advantage that made you more interested or slightly more knowledgeable about your topic.

Aim for ONE big idea

What's your point? You have your audience's attention, they know what's in it for *them*, and they know why *you* are talking about this. Now you need to demonstrate your overall point, your overall purpose. When society was developing long-distance communication by using telegraphs, the sender always had to begin with their most important idea because if the connection was ever lost, then at least the receiver would have it. What would you communicate if you didn't have an entire speech? What one point is the biggest takeaway?

Tell 'em what you're gonna tell 'em

What will you be talking about? The audience is going to wonder what they are in for, what they should be listening for. A good rule of thumb about organizing your ideas is *Tell 'em what you're going to tell 'em, tell 'em, and tell 'em what you told 'em*. A Table of Contents in books fulfills this purpose, but how do you do this with a verbal presentation? Just give the audience an idea of your main talking points. This could be a checklist on one of your opening slides, or even playing a call and response with the audience to see what they might think is important or relevant in your topic. Chances are, if you've done a good job preparing them to receive your message, they will hit on some of your main points. If they do not, that gives you more of an opportunity to tailor your presentation to them. Another thing you can do is "check in" with the audience by using summaries. People's minds will wander no matter how interesting your topic is, no matter how good of a speaker you are. Since people can't rewind a live presentation, the speaker needs to do something to help them catch up.

If I'm presenting about the Great Pacific Garbage Patch, I might talk about how it formed in the first place, what it's doing to the environment right now, and finally, what we can do to clean it up in the future. If I make sure to notify the audience when I move onto the next point, they will be able to re-orient themselves if their mind wanders. This only works if you provided a table of contents or checklist for your presentation.

Use these GREAT steps to start your presentation strong:

Get the audience's attention: "There is one place in the ocean where fish eat the equivalent of 55 jumbo jets worth of plastic each year."
Relate your topic to the audience: "You live on an ocean planet, and just like how you would want to know if someone was using your front yard as their personal dumpster, you deserve to know about what's happening right now in the Pacific."
Explain your expertise: "My name is Chris, and ever since my first marine science course in college, I've been learning more about our relationship with the ocean."
Aim for ONE big idea: "The Great Pacific Garbage Patch is the fastest-accelerating environmental threat today."
Tell 'em what you're gonna tell 'em: "We're going to take a look at how the patch was formed, you'll get to see precisely what it's doing to the environment, and we'll see what can be done about it. Let's get started."

Points

Once you're done planning you're opening, you have two big obstacles that may block your path in presenting your ideas. Those are "What do I say?" and "What if I blank out?" The answer to both questions comes from choosing an organizational pattern. An organizational pattern intentionally crafts your ideas so they are easy for the audience to follow and easy for you to generate and remember. You could fill an entire book solely with organizational patterns and how to use them for different kinds of presentations, but let's take a look at a few of the more common ones.

Topical

Topical organization occurs whenever you organize your ideas as mutually exclusive categories. You simply list different types of things to talk about. If your workplace has asked you to train new sales staff, you might teach them about lead generation, how to earn commissions, and phone call techniques. I encourage new presenters to avoid this organization when possible because it's unnecessarily difficult to remember the topics for both you and the audience. In topical organization, the main ideas are not very closely related to each other, so there is nothing about main point 1 (lead generation) to remind you about main point 2 (commissions). That makes it easy to stare at a blank page struggling to come up with ideas and makes it more likely you could blank out midway through the presentation. I point out this type of organization here because topical organization is what we tend to default to when we start preparing a presentation. We think in terms of lists, categories, and types. Try to notice when you are doing this and take a moment to ask yourself if topical organization is really the best way to approach your topic. The other patterns are so intuitive and easy it will almost feel like cheating.

Chronological

Chronological organization structures our ideas in time. This strategy is incredibly flexible and easy to use. It will feel like your points are being written for you, and when you present, it will feel like you have a little microphone in your ear reminding you of what your next point is. If you have to give a presentation to a new group of sales staff, you could talk about the sales techniques that first got your company started, the sales techniques that are working now, and the sales techniques that are likely to work for future customers. Past, Present, Future. This type of presentation makes it virtually impossible to blank out on while speaking. Here is an example of a more detailed breakdown of ordering sales techniques with a chronological organization.

Entirely in the past: Distant Past, Past, Today
- Sales techniques that were effective at the company's beginning,
- sales techniques that were effective in the early 2000s,
- and sales techniques that are performing well today.

Entirely in the future: Today, the Future, the Distant Future
- Sales techniques that are working today,
- how social media will be shaping our strategies over the next five years,
- and how technology will change our approach over the next 30 years.

Small-scale: First Step, Second Step, Third Step
- How to conduct outbound lead generation through the phone,

- how to close a deal in a conversation,

- and how to get referrals from a happy client.

Spatial

Spatial organization is just as helpful and flexible as chronological organization, but it is not quite as obvious to the audience. Spatial organization occurs when you organize your ideas by their physical location. While a chronological strategy has you think about ideas that come first, second, and third, a spatial approach has you think more in terms of left, center, and right; or top, middle, and bottom. Just as a chronological approach can be large scale, like over the course of many years, or small scale, like the steps you could take in a single day, spatial organization can also be thought of on a large or small scale.

Large-scale: Left, Center, Right
- Sales techniques that have worked best for our clients in Japan,

- techniques that have worked best for our clients on the West Coast,

- and techniques that have worked best for our clients on the East Coast.

Large-scale: Top, Middle, Bottom
- Sales techniques that have helped us grow in Canada,
- sales techniques that have helped us grow in the US,
- and sales techniques that have helped us grow in Mexico.

Small-scale: Left, Center, Right
- The perfect workspace for a sales agent needs to have a computer on your left,
- open space in the middle of your desk for tasks as they arise (and a sociopetal way to speak to clients in front of you),
- and a phone to your right that's out of the way but easy to answer quickly.

Problem-Solution-Outcomes

This organizational pattern is especially useful for motivating change and getting people on board with a new idea or behavior. When we want the audience to do something, it's not enough to tell them our argument and give them reasons why they should believe us. By default, an audience isn't going to be particularly interested in the problems you're trying to solve or why they should be on board. This isn't because they are apathetic, indifferent, or hostile, but because everyone is already attending to a myriad of problems in their own sphere of attention. The Problem-Solution-Outcomes organizational pattern begins by articulating a problem in the world of your audience. Charles Kettering, the former head of research at GM, famously said that "A problem well-stated is a problem half-solved." Articulating the audience's problem better than they can should occur in the first third of your presentation. When you do, they will more than likely assume you have the answer, which sets you up for the rest of your talk.

The solution phase occurs when you present your argument. Most inexperienced speakers try to change the audience's mind by only doing this part. You will succeed where they fail because you have created space for the idea you want to present. No use trying to convince someone to go to the doctor if they don't think they are sick. No need to scratch if there is not an itch. The solution step is where you provide the scratch to the audience's itch. You need to turn your argument into a solution for the audience's problem.

The outcomes phase occurs when you show the emotional benefits of the great things we gain by adopting your idea, or the losses we incur by failing to adopt your idea. Whether you dangle the carrot or wave the stick depends on your style as a speaker, your audience, your topic, or some combination of those factors. Nonetheless, it's important to show us the results, not just lay out the logical reasons to take on an idea you present.

Problem: You are leaving money on the table by focusing solely on outbound lead generation and neglecting inbound lead generation.

Solution: We need to set up a stronger referral system.

Outcomes: A stronger referral system will allow you to bring in more revenue and enjoy more free time.

TOO

For the end of the talk, your exit, what do you do? It's important to ease the audience out of the speech and offer them closure. The conclusion is going to have three parts.

Tell 'em what you told 'em

The first thing you want to do is tell them what you told them. To cement your points in the audience's minds, reiterate your main points and takeaways. To you as the presenter, it's going to feel redundant because surely people already know your points—you just said them. But you would be surprised how even just a few minutes is enough time for ideas to get cluttered in the minds of the audience. You want to make sure all those dots connect.

Offer a takeaway

Once you recap, go back to the most important part of your presentation: the audience. You want to bring the attention back to them because if there's no benefit for them, there's no point in talking. Bring in the moral of your story, the final lesson, the big takeaway. Maybe there's something we never used to see before that we now see. Maybe there's something we used to take for granted that we can now appreciate, or maybe there's something we never used to do that we can do now. Bring it home for the audience.

Own your exit
Finally, you need a nice, solid exit that will cue applause signaling the presentation is over. There are a few different ways to do this, and it might feel a bit intimidating, but there's a trick you can use that is borderline cheating. Bring it back to the attention getter. Have your closing lines allude to your opening lines. It works to your advantage because we're burnt out and just went fishing for a conclusion, but your audience thinks it looks like a clean connection. To the audience, it's going to seem like you had that planned *all along*. Little do they know we're just scraping the bottom of the barrel of our creativity. Joking aside, remember that humans like symmetry. Balancing the end of your speech by pulling from your beginning adds symmetrical organization to your presentation.

If, at the start of your talk, you grabbed the audience's attention with a story, you can give us the ending of that story. If you give us a quote, bring it back. It won't feel redundant because your presentation added more context which gives it more meaning.

Use these tools as a blueprint or outline so you know you're not making things up as you go along. Make sure you use full sentences for each part of the process. You don't want your presentation to sound like you are reading from a page, but make sure you have enough so you know exactly what idea you want to unpack as you talk. You have your plan, and you have GREAT Points TOO.

Supporting Materials

Visual Aids

Pitfalls

If you decide to use visual aids to help the audience keep track of your ideas, be wary of three common pitfalls. Don't worry—there are also six things you can do to make sure these visual aids really work. The three pitfalls: too much text, the speaker using a slide to escape the audience, and visuals upstaging, stealing away attention from the speaker.

Text overload

In the case of too much text, I am sure you have seen slides covered in paragraphs of text. It comes up on screen, and you know this is going to be rough. Rumor has it, Jeff Bezos of Amazon made it a rule for his business meetings that there should be no slide shows.

Text heavy slides challenge the audience to read faster than the speaker can talk. If they get ahead of the speaker, then they no longer care. Worse, the speaker may be tempted to read from the slide. Text overload will tank a presentation in no time at all. Death by PowerPoint.

Being too focused on the slides

In my teaching and coaching, I have seen too many presentations where the speaker glances back at their slide even though nothing useful is there. This tendency is so pernicious

PREPARE EXCEPTIONAL PRESENTATIONS   227

that when I train speakers to present, I will fill a practice presentation with blank slides, and they *still* glance back even though the slides serve no purpose. Your presentation is a conversation. You want to be conversational with the audience in the same way you would speak to a friend. You just happen to have more friends in the audience.

If you stare at your slides, it's exactly like trying to hold a conversation with someone staring at their phone the whole time. You lose that spark. You lose rapport with the person. It's not a conversation anymore. Don't escape your audience by losing yourself in your visuals.

This is more relevant depending on if your presentation is in person and where your slides are. For most presentations, your slides will be on the screen behind you. If you turn away from your audience, your volume is effectively muted. The audience cannot hear you as well.

There's another less obvious reason why volume is so important. It's more of a trade secret. You want your volume to command a presence in the room. You want to be the attention grabber in that space. Even if everyone in the audience were to hold their own phone in front of them with their favorite social media app open, your energy, volume, and voice needs to be dynamic enough to pull their attentions away from their screens and back to you. The director and entertainer, Ken Weber, in his book *Maximum Entertainment*,[70] suggests that even if a speaker has been theatrically trained to use their voice to be heard by hundreds in a room, they should still use a microphone when the audience hits around fifty people. The microphone's added volume allows you to control the energy in a room. Think of how your favorite standup comedian might wait until the laughter of a joke peaks, and just as the laughter starts to fall off, they throw in a second punchline that compounds the laughter even more. That kind of strategy wouldn't be possible without the acoustic gravitas created by the microphone.

If you're offered a microphone, don't pass it up just because people can hear you. The goal isn't to be heard, it's to command a presence. Use the microphone. If you don't have a mic, project your voice through the back of the room, past the back row. Fill the room with your voice. If a 1 is not enough energy, a 3 is too much energy, and a 2 is just right, aim for a 2.5. Use your volume to command a presence.

Upstaging visuals

It is a painful experience for the audience when your slides upstage you as the speaker. You want to avoid pictures that are provocative, gory, or crazy psychedelic because they're going to steal the audience's attention away from you. Ideally, you want to use images that are easy to look at, so we can glance at them and then look back to you. Easy images on the audience's eyes help speakers.

For color schemes, you want to be especially aware of your backgrounds and your fonts. If you have a light-colored background, you want a dark-colored font for contrast. Contrast is the name of the game. If you have a dark-colored background, you want a light-colored font, so it's easy to see. There's no reason to have a blue background and purple font. There's no reason to have a white background and yellow font. It doesn't make any sense. You want to keep that contrast there, and be very deliberate about the kinds of images that you're using.

When you present, you and your slides compete for the audience's attention. You need to win that competition. You have every ability, every advantage against a static slide that can't move, that can't talk, and that can't make a connection with your audience. To help keep your slides from upstaging you, keep the lights on. Don't present in the dark where your screen literally becomes the brightest thing in the room.

When you present, avoid text overload, escaping your audience by diving into the visuals, and make sure your visuals don't shine brighter than you.

Tips

We know the *don'ts*, so what are the *dos*?

Abbreviate ideas

Abbreviate your ideas. Imagine you only have a chalkboard as your visual aid. Without the speed and glam technology offers us, a chalkboard forces us to write by hand. You need to be economic in what you put down and what you don't. Using a chalkboard forces you to highlight your keywords while your speech fills in the blanks. If it's too long to write by hand, do not put it on your slide. *Slides are for glancing, not for reading* (by you or the audience). Remember, the audience will either read your slides or they will listen to you—they will not do both.

If you struggle to keep your ideas short, remember the 8x8 Rule, which suggests you want to go no more than eight words across your slide and no more than eight lines down your slide. As long as you're within that eight-by-eight grid, then you should be all right. Personally, I don't care for the 8x8 Rule because it's still too cluttered for my taste. I keep more to a 4x4 Rule. Less is more.

Use large fonts

Use large fonts. It is better for your fonts to be too readable than not readable enough. Fonts between size ten and size twenty are too small. You want your fonts in the thirties, forties, or more. Remember, we should be glancing, not reading.

Use only a few ideas per slide

One idea equals one slide. Making a new slide for a new idea is free. This might mean you have a lot of slides, but it will be a quick and smooth experience for your audience.

Use the occasional blank slide

Include a blank slide to steal attention back to you. One way that you might steal attention back is every once in a while, when you feel like your slides have made their point and we don't actually need them at the moment, you can include a blank, black slide and our attention will cut back to you. In the exact same way that a TED Talk has the camera mostly on the speaker, but occasionally cuts away to the graph or the image that they have on the slides, but then cuts right back to them; you could do the exact same thing too. The moment your slides cut to black, the attention goes back to you. You are the star of the show. There's no such thing as a PowerPoint presentation, there is only a You presentation.

PREPARE EXCEPTIONAL PRESENTATIONS

Skip the bibliography slide

Please do not end on a bibliography slide. Leave it out. It's best practice to cite sources as you speak instead of saving it for the end. A good way to do this is to incorporate the source in your sentence: "A recent Gallup poll found that 23% of people don't like being slapped by monkeys." It's easy.

A bibliography is not a strong exit. A punchy conclusion with an action step sticks with your audience, a bibliography doesn't. You want the audience to buzz with your presentation as they leave. A bibliography is a buzz killer.

There is an exception to this tip: if you leave your slides with the audience, then keep it—but don't present it, and, even then, it's better to give that bibliography as a handout. Slides help people hang on to your ideas as you speak in real time. A handout exists for an audience that has already left your presentation. Slides are glanceable and minimal, handouts are more thorough and would include a bibliography.

Set up and test everything early

Murphy's Law doesn't care if this is your big day. If something can go wrong, it will go wrong. Show up early and test your presentation. The audience should not be involved in your first draft of this. What makes a good speech isn't having everything go perfectly. It's being okay even when things don't go perfectly because that is how familiar you are with your presentation.

We reviewed three common pitfalls for visual aids, and we covered six tips to help you succeed with visual aids. If you implement these things, then even you can impress meeting planners who would otherwise ban slideshows.

Evidence

Evidence is really important for separating opinions from facts because you want to be seen as a credible speaker. The thing about credibility is that no one *has* credibility. You have eye color, you have fingernails, but you don't have credibility. Credibility is what the audience gives you through their perceptions, and the best way to earn that credibility is to use evidence well.

Imagine your presentation is about tofu. You're not just going to be telling us about your topic from your own personal experience and that one time you made tofu. You're going to bring in research. You're going to cite food scientists that talk about tofu's biochemistry. If you become comfortable understanding the four different types of evidence, it's going to make your research for future projects so much easier. This is going to turn about two hours-worth of research into thirty minutes.

This section covers four types of evidence: examples, stories, testimonials, and statistics.

An **example** is any single case that represents a larger group of cases. If my presentation is about cars, and my main point is about tires, I might say that having good treads on tires makes them safe. That's a nice idea, but how do I prove it? I might use an example by naming a specific kind of tire with really good treads that won it a high safety rating. That one tire with good treads now represents all other tires with good treads via example.

If you're using a **story**, you're actually unpacking an example into a narrative. Let's return to my tire example. This time, I tell the story of a family who took a road trip for their vacation, and how they had to swerve to narrowly avoid a dog in the middle of the road. They spun out of control, but they were okay because they had really good treads on their tires. Even though it serves the same function as the example, I'm using their story and its outcome to prove that tires with treads are safer.

A **testimonial** relies on the expertise of an individual. You use testimonials when you quote an expert. It could be an engineer that designed the tires or a scientist who describes how treads maximize friction on the road. You say treads on tires make them safer, but the audience does not have to take your word for it if you use a testimonial.

Statistics are a very common type of evidence and what most people probably envision when evidence is mentioned. Statistics are number-based facts and include percentages, study results, census results, data surveys, and more.

No type of evidence is better or worse than another. In fact, you shouldn't rely on just one. Your argument becomes stronger when you use a combination of evidence types because each type has their strengths and weaknesses that you must anticipate.

Examples are really good at personalizing abstract ideas. If you include examples of local businesses that sell safe tires, then your audience will relate to that. But if you only ever use examples, then a skeptical audience might think you are cherry-picking evidence. Including statistics in your argument will help negate that impression.

Stories are great at persuading people. You can appeal to their fears, their compassion, and their hope through stories.

But if you only ever use stories, we're faced with the same pitfall of the skeptical audience. You want to show that your story is representative of other cases by using additional types of evidence.

Testimonials are great because they're pretty versatile and easy to find. If you're paraphrasing a testimonial by putting someone's idea in your own words, it is still their idea. For example, a direct quote might be one that's often attributed to Gandhi, like, "An eye for an eye leaves the whole world blind."[71] Even though this is presented as a direct quote, you can paraphrase by saying *Gandhi taught us that violence will only ever create more violence*. Same idea, just your own words. You still need to cite testimonials you're paraphrasing.

When you use testimonials, whether directly or by paraphrasing, you want to make sure they are qualified to talk about your subject. Even if they are qualified, you have to watch out for bias. Just because somebody is educated on a subject doesn't mean they are objective. They might have skin in the game or a dog in the fight.

For example, if you have a topic that's very politically charged, and you are only ever citing Tucker Carlson from Fox News, your presentation will be biased towards the conservative right. The same thing happens in the opposite direction if you only cite Rachel Maddow from MSNBC. If your citations are biased, you will undermine your credibility in the audience's minds.

Generally, statistics are helpful in that they're versatile, easy to find, and rely on numbers. They can be conveyed through forms, surveys, percentages, studies, and more, but we need to avoid overwhelming the audience with numbers.

PREPARE EXCEPTIONAL PRESENTATIONS 235

As humans, we're not very numerate. In the same way someone can be literate or illiterate, a person can be numerate or innumerate. It's because numbers are abstract. It's not because we're dumb. Our brains simply didn't really evolve for abstractions like numbers and calculus. We evolved for tangible concreteness, like recognizing landmarks.

Let me give you an example. In your head, you could probably visualize three bananas pretty comfortably. We have a harder time if we have to imagine seven bananas. In our minds, we probably just see a pile of bananas. We have no hope, then, if we try to visualize 37 bananas, 46 bananas, 12,802 bananas. I certainly can't see that. We understand what the numbers are, but we can't *see* them. If we start overwhelming our audience with numbers and abstractions, after a while, their eyes glaze over. If you use a statistic, relate it to something concrete for the audience, something they can see.

For example, a statistic I might use when discussing the Great Pacific Garbage Patch is that it is around 270,000 square miles large. Our brains cannot compute how big this actually is. We cannot see it in our heads. We just nod along, pout, and think "huh, sounds big." But if I relate the number to something the audience can understand, the point will be made.

One of the tools you can use to help do this is a website called Wolfram Alpha.[72] It's a calculator powered by the Internet where you can do all kinds of fun things like ask it to calculate the height of Barack Obama divided by the age of the universe, and it will tell you the answer (it's 4.3×10^{-18} meters per second, if you were wondering). For our purposes, you can take your statistic, put it in the search box, and it will tell you different ways to convey that statistic. For our Garbage Patch example, I would tell my audience that 270,000 square miles is twice the size of Germany. People's jaws drop when that number is contextualized because the comparison is something tangible, they can feel it. That's two Germany's worth of garbage. This strategy works for all kinds of statistics.

Four different types of evidence, each with their own little quirks. If you're using examples and stories, the big takeaway is you want to make sure that they are representative to the audience, that you're not just cherry-picking single cases that happen to prove your point. If you're going to be using testimonials, make sure they're qualified sources and for the most part, not biased. When you use statistics, make sure you convert those numbers into tangible comparisons the audience can relate to.

Knowing these types of evidence can streamline your future projects. Instead of typing our keywords in a Google search and sifting through pages of results for hours, we can think about what type of evidence you want to include and search specifically for that instead. For example, if for my Garbage Patch presentation, I want to include a statistic about the impact of garbage patches on fish, I search that, and find a study from the Scripps Institution of Oceanography at UC San Diego,[73] which found fish in the area will collectively eat up to 24,000 tons of plastic per year—that's 55 jumbo jets worth of plastic. I plug the statistic (and concrete translation) into the outline, and I'm on to the next part.

10 Tips on Preparing Presentations

1. Use GREAT Points TOO

Get the audience's attention, **R**elate your topic to your audience, **E**xplain your expertise, **A**im at one big idea, **T**ell 'em what you're gonna tell 'em, deliver your **Points**, **T**ell 'em what you told 'em, **O**ffer a takeaway, and **O**wn your exit.

2. Hide your structure to sound natural

Use structure to plan your talk, but speak naturally and conversationally. Planning formulaically can be helpful but speaking formulaically is unnatural.

3. Really nail the first and last 30 seconds

If nothing else, commit to remembering exactly how you will start and how you will finish. That way you can both begin with confidence and end with confidence.

4. Always provide a benefit for your audience

There's no point in speaking to a group if there's nothing in it for the group. What's in it for them?

5. Make your slides glanceable, NOT readable

People will read your slides or listen to you. They will not do both. Avoid full sentences. Paragraphs will be prosecuted to the full extent of the law.

6. Don't look at your slides when speaking

Slides are for the audience, not for the speaker. Treat your slides like you would treat your phone in a job interview. Glance at it once? Okay, *maybe* it was really necessary. Keep looking at it? Don't call us, we'll call you.

7. Use facts deliberately to support ideas, not sprinkled in randomly

Facts and numbers don't speak for themselves. Use them to support larger ideas. "Here are some statistics" shouldn't be spoken unless you can tell us the point of those statistics.

8. Use a variety of facts: Stories, Examples, Testimonials, and Statistics

You have lots of options, don't put all your eggs in one basket.

9. Translate numbers into concrete comparisons

"Two hundred and seventy thousand square miles" of garbage in the ocean doesn't mean anything to us. "Two Germanys" worth of garbage in the ocean will help us understand precisely how much garbage that actually is.

10. Don't wing it

The people who wing it the best aren't even doing that. They are good, on-the-spot speakers because they have habituated good organizational thinking from past experience. Get that experience. Prepare. As they say, practice makes *permanent*.

Chapter 9

Build Your Confidence

"We suffer more often in imagination than in reality."

— Lucius Annaeus Seneca

You are scheduled to deliver a big presentation at work, but you're feeling nervous. What can you do about that? Here is a list of symptoms you may sometimes see from someone giving a presentation:

- Sweaty hands
- Shaking hands
- Flushed cheeks
- Pacing back and forth

- Stammering
- Stuttering
- Fidgeting

What do those symptoms tend to indicate? Many may assume nervousness. We probably relate to many of these experiences when we are nervous. However, this list of symptoms are also indicators of *excitement*. These things happen to us when we're overwhelmed with nervousness *and* when we're extremely excited.

The experience of nervousness and the experience of excitement are the same things in the body.[74] The only difference is a mental one. When you develop the ability to flip that mental switch, then you can take all of that energy and adrenaline and use it to empower you. You can turn your *di*stress into *eu*stress.

Distress is any kind of stress that debilitates. It's harmful, it drags us down. Emotions like anxiety, anger, depression, sadness, and nervousness are forms of distress. **Eustress** is a feeling of stress that's empowering, enabling, and helpful.[75] The *eu-* prefix is the same one in euphoria, like over the top happiness. Even though distress is a bad feeling and eustress is a good feeling, they are the same thing in the body.[76]

When you spot what your thoughts are doing, you can start to direct them, which gives you a huge advantage. Suppose there is a pain in your arm. For some of us, that might mean something worrying, like an injury. But if you have that same pain after having spent the day at the gym, that kind of arm pain feels great. It feels like you did something productive because your muscle is getting stronger. Same pain, different contexts. The point of this chapter is to reshape our nervousness into something powerful and productive. Instead of your arms getting stronger, it will be your confidence.

In exercises where I ask students to list their fears, some common themes appear. Many fears are dangerous, like a fear of the dark where we are at a disadvantage, or a fear of creatures, like spiders and snakes. It makes sense—those things posed potential threats to us. We descended from people who were also scared of heights, dead bodies, bugs, and things like that. If our ancestors touched every spider or snake they saw, we probably wouldn't be here. Oddly enough, another common fear is that of public speaking. That fear sticks out because it doesn't quite fit like the others do. At least the other fears make sense because of the immediate threat.

This is a social fear. To a certain extent, we learn our social fears. Remember when you were a kid and you could do things without shame? Kids will run up and down the aisles in grocery stores, will tug on a stranger's shirt, wave "hi," and run away. Kids have to learn social graces like not running up and down hallways, staring at people, and blurting out whatever comes to mind. Humans develop a nervousness whenever we have too much attention on ourselves, but it is possible for us to unlearn it too. Rumor has it, the fear of public speaking shows up more commonly than the fear of death. Because of this, Jerry Seinfeld used to joke that, at a funeral, people would rather be in the coffin than delivering the eulogy.[77] Hopefully, not us.

It is okay to be nervous about a presentation. In fact, an important first step in combatting nervousness is giving yourself permission to be nervous. We're never really going to get rid of it, but we can learn to live with it and to use it. If someone shows up for a presentation, and they say that they are not nervous at all, that's usually worrisome because it means they might not care about the presentation.

Even professional performers get nervous. If you don't know Chris Evans by name, you certainly know his biceps. Chris Evans played Captain America in the blockbuster Marvel films, and he has gone on record with NBC New York that he gets very nervous. "Most actors are saturated in insecurity and I'm no exception—I'm drowning in it," he said. He experiences tons of insecurity before a role. At the time Marvel Studios was casting Captain America, Chris Evans was talking to a therapist for social anxiety. He even turned down the role a few times because he feared the role would tank his career by destroying it or being stuck in it.[78] As he was talking to his therapist, he realized he was starting to make his career decisions based on fear, and he didn't want to do that. He decided he'd go for it, and it worked out well. He's also been able to do other projects like *Knives Out* and *Snowpiercer*.

There are many other celebrities who get nervous. Adele is on record for throwing up behind the scenes at the height of her career during her tours.[79] Even Beyoncé gets stage fright. She was talking to Rolling Stone about the first time she was ever on stage for a school talent show, and she refused to do it. Her teacher encouraged her to perform, and when she went out on stage, her parents said they didn't even recognize her. It was like she became a different person.[80]

Beyoncé describes her confidence, her dancing, her singing, as putting on a different persona—she even gave the persona a name: Sasha Fierce. At a certain point in her life, Beyoncé would become Sasha Fierce in her performances.[81] Sasha Fierce was even the name of one of her albums because, in her mind, Beyoncé is nervous and shy, but Sasha Fierce is confident and strong and bold.

Nervousness happens to the best of us. Focus on getting to know your nerves because then you can start working with them. Of the many techniques and tricks for dealing with nerves, there is one best exercise for becoming comfortable: practice.

Practice helps you get to know those nerves and work with them more than anything else. Like the Greek poet Archilochus said, "We don't rise to the level of our expectations, we fall to the level of our practice." Practice bits of your presentation when you walk your dog, when you cook your food, when you're in the shower. Your ideas are always with you.

Books and courses on public speaking are replete with tips and tricks for nervousness. You may have come across tips like look at the top of people's heads instead of making direct eye contact, practice in front of a mirror, and take deep breaths before you start. There are good tips (i.e., practice) and bad tips (i.e., picture the audience naked). But I think going about your daily life one way, then using a few tips and tricks to summon Johnny-on-the-spot style confidence might be unfair to ask of you. If we want to change our relationship with nerves in presentations, we will need to re-evaluate our relationship with nerves in life. Confidence in presentations will be a happy byproduct. So far, this book has covered communication with other individuals, with groups, and with audiences; now we need to examine the subtlest communication of all: communication with yourself.

Subconscious Self-Talk for Success

Intrapersonal communication is communication with oneself. If you want to examine the mechanics of nervousness, we can glean some insight from the world of Cognitive Behavioral Therapy. CBT is among the most successful forms of self-talk in helping people deal with anxiety, nervousness, and all kinds of distress. CBT has even outperformed pharmaceuticals in treating people with anxiety.[82] It helps us notice our thoughts and shape them towards something more realistic. While we won't be delving too deep into the world of therapy, there are two big principles behind CBT that we can implement to reinvent our self-talk.

Nervousness is a physiological state of arousal. Like a fire, it needs fuel to burn. What fuels our distress? When we know what fuels our distress, we can remove the fuel, tempering the emotion. The first principle to shape your self-talk identifies the fuel. *It's not the events in our lives that cause distress, but our* **thoughts about those events** *that cause our distress.*

Once when I was a kid, I got so excited at conquering a math problem, I pinned the paper to the wall with my pencil. I didn't realize my hand was in the way until it was too late. I didn't realize I had stabbed myself until I saw blood. Then I cried, freaked out, and ran to my parents. It wasn't the actual act of stabbing that freaked me out. Adrenaline masked my pain for a short time, so it wasn't physical pain either. It was only when I looked down and saw the injury that I freaked out because of the meaning I ascribed to it. Thoughts like death, the doctor cutting off my hand, and lead poisoning freaked out my child self. The injury didn't cause my distress, the meaning I ascribed to it did.

Our thoughts move us towards our nervousness. We do have some involuntary responses, like if you cross the street and a car nearly hits you, you're going to feel a flash of anger and adrenaline. After that, every thought you have is up to you. Do you blame the driver's character and get angry, or do you shrug it off and move along? (Remember the fundamental attribution error from Chapter 2?) On presentation day, you may feel a spark of adrenaline as the host introduces you, but it's up to you if it will grow as excitement or nervousness.

Once you're introduced, if you compare yourself to the last speaker, assume the audience will be bored, and think you're going to blank out, then you are actively fueling that nervousness. Successful self-talk allows us to recognize the invisible second step between stimulus and response. Between the event and our distress there is a space for action, which is generally populated with automatic thoughts. These automatic thoughts are important because they determine the nature of our emotional experience.

The second principle of CBT is about paying attention to these **automatic thoughts**. *Our automatic thoughts are distortions of reality*, fueling our emotional state with inaccurate representations of the world around us. Your brain is lying to you to freak you out. If you can spot this happening to you, then you can shift your thoughts back to something more accurate. You can be more deliberate about what emotional experience you cultivate. But why on earth would your brain lie to you?

Suppose you are a Stone Age human out on the savanna doing your hunter-gatherer thing. You hear a rustle in the bushes behind you. You don't know what it is. Maybe it's just the wind or maybe it is a dangerous predator. Let's imagine that no matter what you guess, you're going to be wrong. If you think it's a dangerous predator and run away but it was just the wind, then nothing happens to you. But if you think it's just the wind and it's a predator, then you're dead. You don't make it back home. You and I descended from the ones who ran.

We are biologically hardwired to freak out about things before we understand them. That fight or flight response was vital to help us survive, but the stressors of today are different than the stressors for which we evolved. Humans have been around for some 300,000 years or so, but only about 6,000 of those years have had human *civilization*. That's only 2% of human existence. Every baby born today is expecting the Paleolithic but gets PowerPoint.

We have the same hardware that helped us survive in the Stone Age, but we've only had a short time to deal with things like job interviews, SATs, traffic, taxes, and presentations. Modern-day stressors are not the same stressors our minds are designed for. Your brain was designed to keep you alive but not to keep you happy, and it's been doing that extremely well with automatic thoughts—distorting your world so you will freak out and survive. In particular, your brain uses ten common **cognitive distortions**. Once you start spotting these cognitive distortions, you are going to have a huge advantage in shaping your experience between stimulus and response, allowing you to transform nervousness into excitement.

The 10 Thoughts Stealing Your Confidence

All-or-Nothing Thinking is especially dangerous for perfectionists. This is the black-and-white thinking when we judge things in complete absolutes. Either my presentation is going to be great, the heavens will part, and the angels will sing; or it's going to bomb, I'm going to ruin my reputation, people are going to hate me, they're going to laugh at me, and I'm going to be remembered as the dumbest speaker of all time. If that sounds familiar, you might have crossed paths with all-or-nothing thinking. This is the kind of thinking that snubs an A-grade for practically being an F.

As we combat these distortions, we're not going to try to fool ourselves by inventing some kind of fake positivity. We need to look at our thoughts objectively and interrogate how realistic or plausible they are. Total success or total failure ignores a lot of other possibilities in the middle. Your presentation turning out "good" or "fine" are valid options. If you ever catch yourself experiencing all-or-nothing thinking, be skeptical of it. Look for the other possibilities because they're probably not so bad, and they're probably more likely to happen.

Overgeneralization occurs whenever we take one negative experience and use it to represent all other experiences. Maybe you did poorly on a presentation, and now you think you will do poorly on all future presentations. You can't take one data point to be representative of all other data points. If you date one person and that person is a jerk, you don't then go around saying that all people are jerks. One data point is just that, one data point.

Mental Filtering focuses only on the negative things we experience while ignoring positive and neutral experiences. We dwell on the negative details. The battle cry of the pessimist is "I'm not a pessimist, I'm a realist." But true realists consider all data points, not just the negative ones. After a presentation, you may internalize that you're bad because you forgot your conclusion's summary. If we punish ourselves for the things we did poorly, then we also have to celebrate the things that we did well or just okay. Even if you forgot your summary, maybe you had a great intro. That's awesome. You also have to give yourself credit for those things to truly be a realist.

Disqualifying the Positive is especially dangerous for smart people. Let's say that we have a mental filter and only the bad stuff comes through. Then a *few* good things come through. Disqualifying the positive is when we rationalize those positive experiences to convince ourselves they don't count. The smarter you are, the better you will be at rationalizing away the good experiences. If you just finished your presentation, are walking back to your seat, and someone says you did a great job, it's easy for you to think they were just being nice. If we filter out nearly all the positive stuff and then splash cold water on what remains, no wonder we feel bad all the time.

Cognitive distortion number five is a two-parter. Five altogether is about jumping to conclusions but in two different ways. Distortion 5a jumps to conclusions by **Mind Reading**. This is when we think we know what other people are thinking, and of course, it's always bad. They are always judgmental. If someone glances at their phone, we know it's because they hate us, and they're texting our friend about their hatred. This is an extremely unlikely scenario, but it doesn't stop us from thinking it. It's also easy to add negative emotions to resting faces. People can't be energetic all the time. Do you always have a smile on, or do you have a resting face too? When presenting you will be in the unique circumstance of seeing far more resting faces than in any other sphere of your life. It is entirely possible for a person to be hooked on your every word in your presentation, to be riveted, listening carefully, and still rest their head on their hand with a flat expression. Different audiences have different energies. Some are noisy and playful, some are quiet. Whenever you see a resting face, don't add to first impressions. Like David Foster Wallace said, "You'll worry less about what people think about you when you realize how seldom they do."

Distortion 5b jumps to conclusions by **Fortune-Telling**. We know what's going to happen and it's going to be bad. We're hyperventilating. We're freaking out. We're feeling our sweaty palms and knowing we're going to pass out. Unless you have a history of fainting when nervous, it's highly unlikely this is going to happen. Just because we have a thought doesn't mean that we have to believe it.

Catastrophizing occurs when we exaggerate all the negative consequences of what's going to happen to us. We start blowing things out of proportion, making them catastrophic. If we forget our summary, then that means we have bad organization, which means the speech will be bad, which means we lose our job, and we'll be homeless. The chain of events is highly unlikely. Even if something did go terribly wrong, what is the worst that would actually happen? You're not going to get fired for forgetting your summary. Your boss may give you constructive feedback about forgetting a summary (if they even notice that at all). Be skeptical of catastrophizing thoughts.

Emotional Reasoning occurs whenever we use our feelings as evidence for a conclusion. If you're waiting for your turn to present, your hands shake, and you conclude you are nervous, therefore, not ready to speak, you used your emotions as evidence. But we can't trust emotions, they are caused by distortions. They are bodily responses to Stone Age threats in our environment and not useful as data. It is entirely possible to be *both* nervous *and* prepared for your presentation. Not only is it possible, it's common. This also translates to things like relationships. It is possible to be angry at our spouse even though they've done nothing wrong. It is possible for us to feel guilty and ashamed even if we have done nothing wrong, but it's so common to attribute anger to wrongdoing even when nobody did anything wrong. We cannot trust our feelings because they are caused by distortions.

Should Statements are the root of our frustration and anger. There cannot be anger without "should." A should statement operates on how we feel things ought to be. When they are not that way, and we feel they should be, we become distressed. As they say, "Expectations are premeditated resentments."

What *should statements* ignore is that there is no one way a thing "should" be. Things are as they are, and if our expectations don't match reality, then our expectations are unrealistic. Maybe I'm getting ready for a virtual presentation, and my webcam dies. It should be working, so I become angry at it instead of accepting the reality of it not working.

Let's *can* our *shoulds*. We can remember that there is a way that things *can* be, not necessarily a way things *should* be. Perhaps it's true that my webcam *can* work as I would prefer, but it is not true that my webcam *should* work as I prefer. Imposing my expectations upon my webcam simply sets me up for frustration. It would be nice if my webcam worked perfectly, but it isn't—now I am free to move on to the next right action.

Labeling occurs whenever we ascribe a judgment to a situation or a person (including ourselves) instead of being descriptive. If we have a bad experience with presentations, we label ourselves as a bad speaker. That's just who you are now. But what even is a "bad speaker"? That's not a thing that exists in nature. Nature doesn't create "bad speakers." Nature creates ants, oceans, clouds, and smelly corpse plants. There may be speakers who do certain things, like say *um* frequently, but that's a habit, not a bad a speaker. Bad is an opinion. It's a label we slap on.

Labeling makes us lazy. It stops us from making progress because the moment I call myself a bad speaker after my fiftieth *um*, I give myself permission to give up because I can't help saying *um*. What if you removed the judgement labels from your vocabulary? What if you were only *descriptive* without being judgmental, and you only described things as they were. Instead of a "bad speaker," you become "someone who says *um* more than they prefer." You can do something about that. You can replace *um* with purposeful pausing or remove them entirely. If you just say that you're a bad speaker, that gives you an excuse to stop improving. Don't judge something as good or bad. Describe the situation and think about what action you can take to achieve what you want.

When we get jittery before a presentation, we say we *are* nervous. No. You have nervousness. Nervousness will arise and it will pass away. If you get sick, you don't say that you *are* fever. You *have* a fever. You're still you. Fevers arise, then they pass away. You don't *become* mosquito bite; you *have* a mosquito bite. You do not become nervous any more than you become mosquito bite. You might have nervousness or jitters, but they aren't you.

Personalization occurs whenever we start taking too much responsibility for something beyond our control. This is another pitfall for those of us that are perfectionists. We like to take responsibility for everything. Maybe in the middle of our presentation we see somebody's attention wander to their phone. We assume it's our fault for not having enough charisma to keep their attention. Personalization occurs whenever we mistake things we can *influence* for things we can *control*. We can influence quite a few things, but ultimately not control them. Instead, do what the Greek philosopher Epictetus recommended and attach your happiness only to the things you can control. If you can't control it, don't worry about it. The only things you can control are your actions.[83]

So, what does that mean for our purposes, for your presentation? Whether or not you have a good or a bad presentation is actually not under your control. There are a million things that could happen that have nothing to do with you doing the right thing. The room you're presenting in could have a blackout or a beloved colleague of the audience may have just passed away. Captain Jean-Luc Picard put it best, "It is possible to commit no mistakes and still lose. That is not a weakness; that is life."[84] You can *influence* the outcome of your presentation greatly by what you do, but you can do everything right and still fail. This idea may feel depressing at first glance, but in practice it is incredibly liberating.

Your goal is not to give a good presentation. Your goal is to do the kinds of things that lead to a good presentation.

Tie your confidence to your inputs, not your outputs. Things like researching, gathering evidence, putting together a thorough outline, practicing several times, getting feedback, and video recording your practice runs. You control your preparation, which will greatly influence your presentation.

Now that you know the most common cognitive distortions, what can you do with this knowledge? Here's something you can do right now.

Let's say you're having a rough week. There's a bunch of reports you need to submit, you're delivering three presentations, things are crazy at home, things are rough at work, and it's stressful. You can sit down with a piece of paper and draw three columns. The first column on the left side is where you identify your automatic thoughts. Normally we don't even notice we're having these automatic thoughts, but if you take a moment to watch your thoughts, you will start identifying them. Put them in the first column. For the purposes of this exercise, you write down *I'm going to blank out.*

In the second column, identify which of the ten cognitive distortions that thought was. Predicting you're going to blank out is fortune-telling.

In the third column, we form a rational response. This cannot be a fake response. We cannot try to artificially force ourselves to be positive. Toxic positivity creates unattainable, unrealistic expectations for us. Instead, we're going to be a realist, not a pessimist in disguise, but an actual realist. A rational response to our example may look something like this:

"I don't know that I will blank out. I probably can't forget the entire presentation because I love my topic, and I'm interested in it outside of this professional setting. I can practice the parts I struggle with a little more."

That's a real, rational response to our brain's irrational responses. Those irrational responses that show up as automatic thoughts were helpful in the Stone Age because they kept us alive, but today they don't keep us happy. By breaking the automatic, irrational responses down, by identifying them for what they are, and then forming a real rational response, you can clear your mind as you go into stressful situations.

This is useful for presentations, job interviews, preparing for difficult conversations, and more. This exercise is recommended by psychologist David Burns in his book *Feeling Good*, which was one of the first books written about CBT for people outside of the psychology community. Until this book, most all of CBT was just exchanged in academic papers between professionals. Burns had a huge backlog of patients from his own private practice, and many of them were in rough shape. He gave them his book and had them read it, do the exercises, and around 60% of those who did no longer needed an appointment with him. It's pretty amazing. Successful subconscious self-talk had tremendous results for them. It will for you too.

10 Tips on Confidence

1. Pick a number of times to practice

Practicing two or three times is good, five is even better. Having a specific number gives you an attainable benchmark. Remember Archilochus's words: "We do not rise to the level of our expectations. We fall to the level of our practice." The way you practice is the way you will perform.

2. Choose when and where you will practice

Committing to "practice" is abstract. It's imprecise and easy to neglect. Committing to practicing at least once, start to finish, after you've had breakfast, every day for five days, is a concrete goal you can measure.

3. Give yourself permission to be nervous

No need to get nervous about being nervous. If Beyonce´ is allowed to be nervous, you are allowed to be nervous. If you notice some nervousness, just welcome it to the party.

4. Get comfortable being uncomfortable

We are not going to completely eliminate nerves, but we can learn to get along with them, which is a huge advantage.

5. Avoid false positivity

Telling yourself everything is going to be perfect is disingenuous, which prevents you from believing it. You will feel failure even more when something *doesn't* go perfectly. Just don't believe your own false negativity and you'll be alright (and all the negativity is false).

6. Spot your Automatic Thoughts

Identify your automatic thoughts. "I'm going to blank out," "Everyone will be bored," and so on. Just because you have a thought doesn't mean you need to believe it.

7. Identify your Cognitive Distortions

Those automatic thoughts you spot are distortions of reality. What kind of cognitive distortion did you spot? All-or-Nothing Thinking, Overgeneralization, Mental Filtering, Disqualifying the Positive, Mind Reading, Fortune Telling, Catastrophizing, Emotional Reasoning, Labeling, or Personalization? Maybe a combination?

8. Respond to the distortions with rational responses

"I'm going to blank out and everyone will judge me" is distorted and unhelpful. "I probably won't blank out on everything—I'm passionate about this subject. Even if I forget a detail or two, I could steal a glimpse at a slide to remind me. And I don't know for sure how people will react. They'll probably be more interested in the material than in me anyway. That's how I am as an audience member." That response is more realistic and more helpful.

9. Think more about helping your audience than about your reputation

Get interested in your material, not yourself. Wondering what the audience will think of you is unhelpful and, honestly, irrelevant. Focus instead on the audience's needs. "Just wait until they hear the story in my next point, it's a great one!"

10. Get excited

Nervousness is physiologically identical to excitement. Don't tell yourself you're nervous, tell yourself you're excited. As a speaker, you are not in the hot seat, you are in the power seat. You get to craft everyone's experience. What a uniquely rare opportunity that is!

Conclusion

My very first memory is standing in the brown-walled hallway of my grandma's house, frustratedly staring at a point in empty space. I'm about three years old. Up until this point, life has been free. I haven't yet gone to school, gotten a job, or taken on any responsibilities. I walk or run where I want, eat snacks, watch cartoons, pet the dog, stare at bugs—life is good. But mid-step down this hallway, I am frozen. I know I am walking to find a parent or grandparent because I want to express an emotion. I am used to declaring hunger, boredom, or other requests for attention as if everyone needs to hear them. But this time I'm stuck. I'm feeling an emotion and I don't have a word for it. I don't know what I'm going to do or say once I find an adult. Even though I can physically walk or run anywhere I want, I feel trapped. Without more words—like the grown-ups have—I am trapped in my own head.

We are all, to a certain extent, trapped in our own heads. But we gain freedom as we communicate. Your voice is your freedom. The more you express and articulate yourself, the more of your authentic self you can be outside the confines of your own brain. In her book *The Extended Mind*, science writer Annie Murphy Paul poses the thought-provoking question, "Where does your mind end and the rest of the world begin?"[85] We intuitively feel like our mind ends inside of our skull, but Paul points out that much of our thinking takes place outside of our brain. For example, we think through math problems more accurately by gesturing with our hands, we store memories in our surroundings with souvenirs, we create original ideas we would not otherwise generate by talking with others. Our minds are larger than our brains.

Your capacity to communicate is your capacity to expand yourself—to become *more you*. You only get one chance to be you. The number one regret people have on their deathbeds is living a life based on others' expectations as opposed to a life that was true to themselves.[86] We only have one chance to be our fullest, truest selves; but doing that requires being understood, avoiding misunderstanding, improving our relationships, navigating our disagreements, and speaking up even though we're nervous. You have ideas and expertise to share, you have passions and interests the rest of us need to experience, you have relationships to enrich and contributions to make. The more you do these things, the richer and more vibrant the world becomes. That's the world I want to live in. That's the world I want to raise kids in. I hope the tools in this book, in some small measure, help you to escape the confines of your head, empower your voice, and be your fullest, truest self.

Everything in this book is free. There is no charge for using stimuli with higher meme activation potential or avoiding psychological noise so you can be understood. It costs nothing to monitor your own confirmation bias or give others the benefit of the doubt by remembering the fundamental attribution error. There is no gadget you must purchase to keep a 5 to 1 ratio of positive to negative comments with your partner, to replace expressive speech acts with assertives, or to avoid the four horsemen to have a happier relationship. You don't need to download a special app to observe your interactional synchrony when you talk to others, to mind your tone of voice, or move your living room furniture to create sociopetal environments and inspire better conversations. There is no subscription fee to skeptically examine facts, spot a practical-principle clash in a dispute, consider what would change your own mind, sit with some cognitive dissonance, or welcome a new friend into your Monkeysphere. You don't need to take out a loan to prepare GREAT Points TOO in presentations, to make glanceable rather than readable slides, or turn your statistics into concrete comparisons. You don't need to pay shipping or handling before you tune into your subconscious self-talk, spot cognitive distortions, form rational responses, channel your nervousness, and grow your confidence.

You also require no special skills or talents to get started. Everything in this book works for you whether you can't sing, are forgetful, have weak biceps, have no sense of rhythm, or can't swim. You require no muscle memory, conditioning, weigh-in, gifts, or talents to get started. There is zero barrier to entry to begin crafting your communication, but there is so much to gain. Whether you are making a marriage happier, finally being understood, delivering a presentation you can be proud of, or transforming your confidence, you have everything you need to get started *right now*. I couldn't be more excited for you.

Book Recommendations

This book was designed to cover a wide range of communication topics for all walks of life. If you found one particular subject fascinating and would be interested in a deeper dive, here are some books I recommend.

INTERPERSONAL COMMUNICATION

The Seven Principles for Making Marriage Work by John Gottman and Nan Silver
Terrific, hands-on, science-based guide for building and maintaining a relationship that lasts.

Don't Shoot the Dog: The New Art of Teaching and Training by Karen Pryor
Essential reading for anyone trying to shape the behavior of themselves or others. Whether you're dealing with a screaming child, irritating spouse, procrastinating self, or even a

barking dog; this book teaches the fundamental principles of any behavior change.

How to Win Friends and Influence People by Dale Carnegie
An oldie, but a goodie. Not science-driven in its writing, but much of the material has since been validated by communication research and holds up well today.

Give and Take: A Revolutionary Approach to Success by Adam Grant
Is it better to be a giver or a taker? Do nice guys finish last? Learn the surprising truths of reciprocity, relationship building, and more in this terrific well-researched book.

Thinking, Fast and Slow by Daniel Kahneman
This is a big, dense book, but it's among the most authoritative collections of the cognitive biases that lead to our misunderstandings in the world.

PUBLIC DISCOURSE

The Scout Mindset: Why Some People See Things Clearly and Others Don't by Julia Galef
A refreshingly approachable collection of vital ideas and exercises to help us find the truth in a world where everyone is trying to prove a point.

Think Again: The Power of Knowing What You Don't Know by Adam Grant
One of the best books I can recommend on dealing with disagreements. Well-researched and immediately useful.

The Demon-Haunted World: Science as a Candle in the Dark by Carl Sagan
Conversations about what's true or false are difficult, especially when a little mistruth can bring a lot of comfort. Carl Sagan's classic veneration of critical thought is a must-read.

How To Have Impossible Conversations: A Very Practical Guide by James Lindsay and Peter Boghossian
A useful, list-driven, and very approachable book to walk you through difficult disagreements with the people who matter most.

How to be Perfect: The Correct Answer to Every Moral Question by Michael Schur
You would think a fun, approachable book to a topic as dense as moral philosophy couldn't be written. But if anyone can do it, it's Michael Schur, writer for hit shows like *The Office*, *Parks and Recreation*, *The Good Place*, and *Brooklyn Nine-Nine*. You'll laugh and you'll learn.

The Righteous Mind: Why Good People Are Divided by Politics and Religion by Jonathan Haidt
A masterclass in moral psychology. This book is a deep dive that will expand your Monkeysphere like few others can.

PUBLIC SPEAKING

Made to Stick: Why Some Ideas Survive and Others Die by Chip Heath and Dan Heath
Essential reading for anyone who needs their message to "stick." Now that you have the basics of preparing your ideas as a presenter, Made to Stick is the best natural follow-up to help you craft your messages for your audience. Highly recommended.

Switch: How to Change Things When Change Is Hard by Chip Heath and Dan Heath
If you need to change or persuade your audience, not just teach them or share information, this book is the natural follow-up to Made to Stick.

The Memory Book: The Classic Guide to Improving Your Memory at Work, at School, and at Play by Harry Lorayne and Jerry Lucas
Being able to speak without notes, just from memory, is one of the best benefits of good rehearsal. Fast-track your journey there with the definitive guide to memory techniques.

Chatter: The Voice in Our Head, Why It Matters, and How to Harness It by Ethan Kross
A fabulous guide to the self-talk that drives much of our anxiety as speakers.

Meditation for Fidgety Skeptics: A 10% Happier How-to Book by Dan Harris, Jeff Warren, and Carlye Adler
Mindfulness meditation may be the best long-term habit you can adopt for dealing with nervousness. Don't take my word for it, ABC anchor Dan Harris had a panic attack on live TV. His search for solutions led to the creation of this book.

Feeling Good: The New Mood Therapy by David Burns
This book is a very deep dive into distress that may not be for everyone. Whether you're combating nervousness, anxiety, depression, or any other kind of severe distress, this is the definitive lay-person's guide to cognitive behavioral therapy.

If You Enjoyed This Book...

Thank you for reading this book—honestly. This project was a labor of love as an independent author. I don't have the sponsorship deals, employees, or the massive corporate publishers that place books in every airport around the world. This book was my pet project over the pandemic so that my students and professional audiences who found something useful from me could take some of these ideas with them. If you thought any of the ideas in this book could be helpful in your own life or thought someone you know should read it, I'd like to use this page of the book to speak directly to you.

It would make a world of difference if you would consider doing any of the following that is easiest for you:

- Leave a review on Amazon.com

- Leave a review on Goodreads.com

- Recommend the book to a coworker, supervisor, or

employee if you think the ideas would help improve your workplace

- Recommend the book to a friend or family member if you think something in it will help them in life

- Mention this book the next time you comment on your favorite podcast or blog

- Post about this book on Facebook or Twitter

- Take a selfie with the book for Instagram or...dance with it on TikTok (that's what they do on TikTok, right?)

- Get in touch at www.ChristianGilbert.com to let me know what you thought

Even just one of these little actions goes a long way in helping this book find the people for whom it can do the most good. If you thought this book was in any way recommendable, I would deeply appreciate your assistance in connecting it with the people it was meant to help.

Acknowledgements

Coleman, Daniel, Jaynah, Jenna, Kevin, Matt, Michael, Sarah, Spencer, Taryn, Dennis, Sally, Amber, Chris, Ryder, Brayden, Mom, and Dad: Thank you for all of your help and feedback with title ideas, subtitle ideas, and cover feedback. Thank you for all of your support and for asking how the book was coming along, which kept me accountable and forced me to keep working. Thank you all for your enthusiasm during the whole process.

Bobbie, Cindy, Erin, and Nicole: Thank you for the path you paved and the examples you set. Thank you for your support, mentorship, and friendship.

Amy, Kelly, and Krystyna: Thank you for sharing your experience, your expertise, and for your guidance. Thank you for the work you do in advancing this wonderful field that improves the lives of so many.

Matt and Gabe: Thank you for first instilling the idea of writing this book. Thank you for your ongoing support, your niche expertise and guidance, for talking shop at all hours of the day and night no matter the time differences, and excellent taste in hairstyles.

Mimi, Sonja, Kiryl: Thank you for your editing, fact-checking, and design. Your patience with me, your constant revisions, your sharp eyes, and your expertise.

Lucille: Thank you for talking with me every day and bouncing ideas. Thank you for working with me and refining, in one form or another, all the ideas in this book through conversation and through practice for well over a decade. Thank you for your sharp eye, your second opinions, and your enthusiastic interest with this project. Most of all, thank you for using the best of these communication techniques on me, improving my absolute most important relationship. I am fortunate to have such an excellent crafter of communication in my life.

Notes

Introduction

1. **Mars simulation**: Hersher, R. (2016, August 29). "Mars Mission" crew emerges from yearlong simulation in Hawaii. NPR. https://www.npr.org/sections/thetwo-way/2016/08/29/491794937/mars-mission-crew-emerges-from-yearlong-simulation-in-hawaii

2. **Bad news communication**: Back, A. L., & Curtis, J. R. (2002). Communicating bad news. The Western Journal of Medicine, 176(3), 177-180. doi:10.1136/ewjm.176.3.177; More bad news: Sobczak, K., Leoniuk, K., & Janaszczyk, A. (2018). **Delivering bad news**: patient's perspective and opinions. Patient Prefer Adherence, 12, 2397-2404. doi:10.2147/PPA.S183106; **Bad news is difficult to convey**: Alshami, A., Douedi, S., Avila-Ariyoshi, A., Alazzawi, M., Patel, S., Einav, S., Surani, S, Varon, J. (2020). Breaking Bad News, a Pertinent Yet Still an Overlooked Skill: An International Survey Study. Healthcare (Basel, Switzerland), 8(4), 501. doi:10.3390/healthcare8040501; **We're still trying to figure out how to convey bad news well in medicine**: Brewer, J., Bartlett, M., Harris, D., & Hui, C. (2021). Improving communication between healthcare providers and pulmonary arterial hypertension patients: a survey of patient preferences. Pulmonary Circulation,

11(2), 20458940211015813-20458940211015813. doi:10.1177/20458940211015813

3. **Methods vs. Principles**: Pryor, K. (2002). *Don't Shoot the Dog!: The New Art of Teaching and Training*. Interpret Ltd. **For a hilarious success story of how one woman transformed her husband using nothing but the principle of rein_forcement, see What Shamu Taught Me About a Happy Marriage**: Sutherland, A. (2019, October 11) What Shamu Taught Me About a Happy Marriage. *The New York Times*. https://www.nytimes.com/2019/10/11/style/modern-love-what-shamu-taught-me-happy-marriage.html

Chapter 1: Be Understood

4. **Sender-Receiver Model**: *Communication in the Real World* (2016). https://open.lib.umn.edu/communication/

5. **Memetics**: Blackmore, S., & Dawkins, R. (2000). *The Meme Machine*. Oxford; New York: Oxford University Press.

6. **Memes spread**: Dawkins, R. (2019). *The Selfish Gene*. London: Folio Society.

Chapter 2: Avoid Misunderstanding

7. **Grice's Maxims**: Grice, H. P. (1975). Logic and conversation. In *Speech Acts* (pp. 41-58): Brill.

8. **The Traffic Light Rule**: Goulston, M. (2015, June 3). How to know if you talk too much. *Harvard Business Review*. https://hbr.org/2015/06/how-to-know-if-you-talk-too-much. **Original post**: Namko, M. (n.d.). Do You Talk Too Much? MartyNemko.com. Retrieved from https://martynemko.com/articles/do-you-talk-too-much_id1371

9. **Da Kine**: Nosowitz, D. (2017). "'Da Kine,' Hawaii's Fantastically Flexible All-Purpose Noun." Retrieved 11/8/21, 2021, from https://www.atlasobscura.com/articles/da-kine-hawaiian-pidgin.

10. **Speech Acts**: Austin, J. L. (1975). *How to do Things With Words*: Oxford university press.; Searle, J. R., & Willis, S. (2002). *Consciousness and Language*: Cambridge University Press.; Searle, J. R. (1985). *Expression and Meaning: Studies in the Theory of Speech Acts*: Cambridge University Press.; Searle, J. R. (1965). What is a Speech Act. *Perspectives in the Philosophy of Language: a Concise Anthology*, 2000, 253-268.; Nastri, J., Peña, J., & Hancock, J. T. (2006). The construction of away messages: A speech act analysis. *Journal of Computer-Mediated Communication*, 11(4), 1025-1045.

11. **Wason Selection Task**: Wason, P. C. (1968). Reasoning about a rule. *Quarterly Journal of Experimental Psychology*, 20(3), 273-281. doi:10.1080/14640746808400161

12. **Smart people are good at justifying things they came to believe for non-smart reasons**: Shermer, M. (2002). *Why People Believe Weird Things: Pseudoscience, Superstition, and Other Confusions of our Time*: Macmillan.

13. **"Man is not a rational animal, he is a rationalizing animal"**: Heinlein, R. A. (1974). *Assignment in Eternity: By Robert A. Heinlein*. New York: New American Library.

14. **"Lunacy"**: Carroll, R. T. (2015). Full Moon and Lunar Effects. *The Skeptic's Dictionary: From Abracadabra to Zombies*. Retrieved from http://www.skepdic.com/fullmoon.html

15. **Superstition**: Skinner, B. F. (1948). 'Superstition' in the pigeon. *Journal of Experimental Psychology, 38*(2), 168–172. https://doi.org/10.1037/h0055873

16. **Crop circles**: Carroll, R. T. (2015). Crop "circle". *The Skeptic's Dictionary: From Abracadabra to Zombies.* Retrieved from http://skepdic.com/cropcirc.html

17. **"...be angry at the right person, to the right degree, for the right reasons, at the right time, and in the right way..."**: Aristotle, Ross, W. D., & Brown, L. (2009). *The Nicomachean Ethics.* Oxford: Oxford University Press.

Chapter 3: Improve Your Relationships

18. **Heavy-set body types**: Glenton, V. (2016). Plus Size Women Throughout History: Women in the Renaissance. *She Might Be - An Online Plus Size Community.* Retrieved from https://shemightbe.co.uk/plus-size-women-throughout-history-women-renaissance/

19. **Physical attraction symmetry**: Grammer, K., & Thornhill, R. (1994). Human (Homo sapiens) facial attractiveness and sexual selection: the role of symmetry and averageness. *Journal of Comparative Psychology, 108*(3), 233.; **More on symmetry**: Jones, B. C., Little, A. C., Penton-Voak, I. S., Tiddeman, B. P., Burt, D. M., & Perrett, D. I. (2001). Facial symmetry and judgements of apparent health: Support for a "good genes" explanation of the attractiveness–symmetry relationship. *Evolution and Human Behavior, 22*(6), 417-429.; **Cross-cultural attraction**: Rhodes, G., Yoshikawa, S., Clark, A., Lee, K., McKay, R., & Akamatsu, S. (2001). Attractiveness of facial averageness and symmetry in non-western cultures: in search of biologically based standards of beauty. *Perception, 30*(5), 611-625. doi:10.1068/p3123; **More on cross-culture attraction**: Sorokowski, P., Kościński, K., & Sorokowska, A. (2013). Is beauty in the eye of the beholder but ugliness culturally universal? Facial preferences of Polish and Yali (Papua) people. *Evolutionary Psychology, 11*(4),

147470491301100414.

20. **Culture shapes attraction**: Voegeli, R., Schoop, R., Prestat-Marquis, E., Rawlings, A. V., Shackelford, T. K., & Fink, B. (2021). Cross-cultural perception of female facial appearance: A multi-ethnic and multi-centre study. *PloS ONE, 16*(1), e0245998. doi:10.1371/journal.pone.0245998

21. **Hugh Jackman's preparation**: CBS (Producer). (2017, August 2021). Hugh Jackman's Three-Month Prep for a Shirtless Scene. *The Late Show with Stephen Colbert*.

22. **We disclose quickly online**: Joinson, A. N. (2001). Self-disclosure in computer-mediated communication: The role of self-awareness and visual anonymity. *European Journal of Social Psychology, 31*(2), 177-192. doi:https://doi.org/10.1002/ejsp.36

23. **Task attraction**: McCroskey, J. C., & McCain, T. A. (1974). The measurement of interpersonal attraction. *Speech Monographs, 41*, 261-266.

24. **Love Styles**: Lee, J. A. (1973). *Colours of love: An Exploration of the Ways of Loving*: New Press.

25. **Social Exchange**: Thibaut, J. W., & Kelley, H. H. (1959). *The Social Psychology of Groups*. New York, NY: Wiley.

26. **The Gottmans**: A great everyday guide to implementing the research from marriages into one's own life is Gottman, J. (2018). *The Seven Principles for Making Marriage Work*: Hachette UK.

27. **Predicting divorce accurately**: This classic, original study is Buehlman, K.

T., Gottman, J. M., & Katz, L. F. (1992). How a couple views their past predicts their future: Predicting divorce from an oral history interview. *Journal of Family Psychology*, 5(3-4), 295.

Chapter 4: Learn the Truth About Lie-Detection

28. **Defining deception**: Vrij, A. (2001). Psychology of Deception. In N. J. Smelser & P. B. Baltes (Eds.), *International Encyclopedia of the Social & Behavioral Sciences* (pp. 3278-3281). Oxford: Pergamon.

29. **Falsification, Omission, Equivocation, and Misdirection**: McCornack, S. A. (1992). Information manipulation theory. *Communications Monographs*, 59(1), 1-16.; **Testing IMT**: McCornack, S. A., Levine, T. R., Solowczuk, K. A., Torres, H. I., & Campbell, D. M. (1992). When the alteration of information is viewed as deception: An empirical test of information manipulation theory. *Communications Monographs*, 59(1), 17-29.

30. **Meta-analysis of deception "tells"**: DePaulo, B. M., Lindsay, J. J., Malone, B. E., Muhlenbruck, L., Charlton, K., & Cooper, H. (2003). Cues to deception. *Psychological Bulletin*, 129(1), 74.

31. **Training doesn't help lie-detection**: Levine, T. R., Feeley, T. H., McCornack, S. A., Hughes, M., & Harms, C. M. (2005). Testing the effects of nonverbal behavior training on accuracy in deception detection with the inclusion of a bogus training control group. *Western Journal of Communication*, 69(3), 203-217.

32. **We're about 55% accurate at lie-detection**: Bond Jr, C. F., & DePaulo, B. M. (2006). Accuracy of deception judgments. *Personality and Social Psychology*

Review, 10(3), 214-234.

33. **The difficult exam metaphor**: Levine, T. R. (2010). A few transparent liars explaining 54% accuracy in deception detection experiments. *Annals of the International Communication Association*, 34(1), 41-61.

Chapter 5: Read People

34. **"You see, but you do not observe"**: Doyle, A. C., & Paget, S. (1891). *A Scandal in Bohemia*. London: G. Newnes.

35. **Facial expressions**: Ekman, P., & Friesen, W. V. (1971). Constants across cultures in the face and emotion. *Journal of Personality and Social Psychology*, 17(2), 124.; **More on cross-cultural facial expressions**: Ekman, P. (1989). The argument and evidence about universals in facial expressions. *Handbook of Social Psychophysiology*, 143, 164.

36. **Walks can be more or less attractive**: Fink, B., Andre, S., Mines, J., Duverge Castillo, B., Shackelford, T., & Butovskaya, M. (2016). Sex difference in attractiveness perceptions of strong and weak male walkers. *American Journal of Human Biology*, 28. doi:10.1002/ajhb.22891

37. **Proxemics**: Hall, E. T. (1961). *The Hidden Dimension*. New York; Doubleday: Anchor Books.

38. **Haptics**: Heslin, R. (1974). Steps toward a taxonomy of touching. Paper presented to the annual meeting of the Midwestern Psychological Association, Chicago, IL.

39. **"Life finds a way"**: Spielberg, S. (1993). *Jurassic Park*. Universal Pictures. Yup,

I cited a dinosaur movie in a communication book. Someone had to do it.

40. **The famous "Midas Touch" study**: Crusco, A. H., & Wetzel, C. G. (1984). The Midas Touch: The Effects of Interpersonal Touch on Restaurant Tipping. *Personality and Social Psychology Bulletin*, 10(4), 512-517. doi:10.1177/0146167284104003

41. **Self-oriented and other-oriented identity claims**: Gosling, S. (2009). *Snoop: What Your Stuff Says About You*. New York: Basic Books.

42. **Compatible immune systems**: Thornhill, R., Gangestad, S. W., Miller, R., Scheyd, G., McCollough, J. K., & Franklin, M. (2003). Major histocompatibility complex genes, symmetry, and body scent attractiveness in men and women. *Behavioral Ecology*, 14(5), 668-678.

43. **Citrus smells made people tidier**: Holland, R. W., Hendriks, M., & Aarts, H. (2005). Smells like clean spirit: Nonconscious effects of scent on cognition and behavior. *Psychological Science*, 16(9), 689-693.

Chapter 6: Talk About What's True

44. **The Pareto Principle**: Koch, R. (2011). *The 80/20 Principle: The Secret of Achieving More with Less: Updated 20th anniversary edition of the productivity and business classic*: Hachette UK.

45. **Josh Kaufman plays the ukulele with only four chords**: TEDx Talks. (2013, March 14). *The first 20 hours -- how to learn anything | Josh Kaufman* [Video]. YouTube. https://www.youtube.com/watch?v=5MgBikgcWnY

46. **The Dress**: McCoy, T. (2015, February 27). The inside story of the 'white dress, blue dress' drama that divided a planet. *The Washington Post*.

https://www.washingtonpost.com/news/morning-mix/wp/2015/02/27/the-inside-story-of-the-white-dress-blue-dress-drama-that-divided-a-nation/ **It caused drama for the family who first found it**: Benedictus, L. (2015, December 22). #Thedress: 'It's been quite stressful having to deal with it...we had a falling out'. *The Guardian*. https://www.theguardian.com/fashion/2015/dec/22/thedress-internet-divided-cecilia-bleasdale-black-blue-white-gold

47. **"I think, therefore I am"**: Descartes, R. (1999). *Discourse on Method and Meditations on First Philosophy*: Hackett Publishing.

48. **You don't experience being wrong**: Schulz, K. (2010). *Being wrong: Adventures in the margin of error*. Ecco.

49. **"Keep an open mind, but no so open your brains fall out"**: Farley, T. (2014). A Skeptical Maxim (May) Turn 75 This Week. Retrieved from https://www.skeptic.com/insight/open-mind-brains-fall-out-maxim-adage-aphorism/#note02

50. **The invisible dragon**: Sagan, C. (1997). *The Demon-Haunted World: Science as a Candle in the Dark* (1. Ballantine Books ed). Ballantine Books.

51. **Falsification**: Popper, Karl (1959). *The Logic of Scientific Discovery* (2002 pbk; 2005 ebook ed.). Routledge

52. **Russell's Teapot**: Russell, Bertrand (1952). In Slater, John G. (ed.). *The Collected Papers of Bertrand Russell, Vol. 11: Last Philosophical Testament, 1943–68*. Routledge. pp. 542–548.

53. **The CRAAP Test**: Blakeslee, Sarah (2004) "The CRAAP Test," *LOEX Quarterly*:

Vol. 31 : No. 3 , Article 4. Available at: https://commons.emich.edu/loexquarterly/vol31/iss3/4

Chapter 7: Talk About What's Good

54. **Science means knowledge**: Butler-Adam, J. (2015). The weighty history and meaning behind the word 'science'. *The Conversation*. Retrieved from https://theconversation.com/the-weighty-history-and-meaning-behind-the-word-science-48280

55. **Utilitarianism**: Bentham, J., Burns, J. H., Hart, H. L. A., & Bentham, J. (1996). *An Introduction to the Principles of Morals and Legislation*. Clarendon Press; Oxford University Press.

56. **"The needs of the many outweigh the needs of the few"**: Meyer, N. (1982). *Star Trek II: The Wrath of Khan*: Paramount Pictures.

57. **"The ends justify the means"**: Machiavelli, Niccolò, 1469-1527. (1981). *The Prince*. Harmondsworth, Eng.; New York, N.Y.: Penguin Books.

58. **FBI vs. Apple**: Nakashima, E. (2016, February 17). Apple vows to resist FBI demand to crack iPhone linked to San Bernardino attacks. *The Washington Post*. https://www.washingtonpost.com/world/national-security/us-wants-apple-to-help-unlock-iphone-used-by-san-bernardino-shooter/2016/02/16/69b903ee-d4d9-11e5-9823-02b905009f99_story.html

59. **Thought experiment on abortion**: For the sake of brevity and to not veer too waywardly into subjects beyond the scope of this book, I've used a very oversimplified thought experiment about silly helmets. However, full credit goes to Judith Jarvis Thomson and her original thought experiment about waking up

connected to a sleeping violinist. If this section of the book was of interest to you, I highly recommend digging up and reading the original source: Thomson, J. J. (1976). A defense of abortion. In *Biomedical Ethics and the Law* (pp. 39-54). Springer, Boston, MA.

60. **Our opinions have more in common than we realize**: Kliff, S. (2018, February 2). What Americans think of abortion. Vox. https://www.vox.com/2018/2/2/16965240/abortion-decision-statistics-opinions

61. **Moral Foundations Theory**: Haidt, J., & Joseph, C. (2004). Intuitive ethics: how innately prepared intuitions generate culturally variable virtues. *Daedalus*, 133(4), 55-66. doi:10.1162/0011526042365555; Haidt's collection of research:

62. **A collection of MFT research**: Moral Foundations Theory., Haidt, J., & Dobolyi, D. (2021). Moral Foundations Theory. Retrieved from https://moralfoundations.org

63. **Haidt's TED Talk**: TED-Ed, & Haidt, J. (2013). The moral roots of liberals and conservatives - Jonathan Haidt. Retrieved from https://www.youtube.com/watch?v=8SOQduoLgRw

64. **Brain size and social group size**: Dunbar, R. I. M. (1992). Neocortex size as a constraint on group size in primates. *Journal of Human Evolution*. 22(6): 469–493. doi:10.1016/0047-2484(92)90081-J

65. **The Monkeysphere**: NPR. (2011). Don't Believe Facebook; You Only Have 150 Friends. Retrieved from https://www.npr.org/2011/06/04/136723316/dont-believe-facebook-you-only-have-150-friends

66. **"Them" vs. "Those of us"**: Ferriss, T. (2020). The Tim Ferriss Show Transcripts: Penn Jillette on Magic, Losing 100+ Pounds, and Weaponizing Kindness (#405). Retrieved from https://tim.blog/2020/01/27/penn-jillette-transcript/

Chapter 8: Prepare Exceptional Presentations

67. **"All good public speaking comes from good private thinking"**: Berkun, S. (2010). *Confessions of a Public Speaker*. O'Reilly.

68. **The T-rex lived closer to our time than the time of the stegosaurus**: Black, R. (2012). On Dinosaur Time. *Science*. Retrieved from https://www.smithsonianmag.com/science-nature/on-dinosaur-time-65556840/

69. **Your phone's technology vs. technology to land on the Moon**: Kendall, G. (2019). Would your mobile phone be powerful enough to get you to the moon? *The Conversation*. Retrieved from https://theconversation.com/would-your-mobile-phone-be-powerful-enough-to-get-you-to-the-moon-115933

70. **Use a mic when the audience hits 50**: Weber, K. (2003). *Maximum Entertainment: Director's Notes for Magicians and Mentalists* (1. ed). Ken Weber Productions.

71. **"Eye for an eye"**: Quote Investigator. (2010). An Eye for an Eye Will Make the Whole World Blind. Retrieved from https://quoteinvestigator.com/2010/12/27/eye-for-eye-blind/

72. **Wolfram Alpha**: Retrieved from https://www.wolframalpha.com

Chapter 9: Build Your Confidence

73. **Fish eating up to 24,000 tons of plastic**: Davison, P., & Asch, R. G. (2011). Plastic ingestion by mesopelagic fishes in the North Pacific Subtropical Gyre. *Marine Ecology Progress Series*, 432, 173-180. https://doi.org/10.3354/meps09142

74. **Excitement vs. Nervousness**: This fascinating study found that simply saying to oneself "I am excited" improved performance and perceived performance on stressful tasks like singing in public, giving a presentation, or taking a math test. Brooks, A. W. (2014). Get excited: reappraising pre-performance anxiety as excitement. *Journal of Experimental Psychology: General*, 143(3), 1144.

75. **Eustress**: American Psychological Association. (2021). Eustress. *American Psychological Association Dictionary*. Retrieved from https://dictionary.apa.org/eustress

76. **Distress vs. Eustress**: Bienertova-Vasku, J., Lenart, P., & Scheringer, M. (2020). Eustress and Distress: Neither Good Nor Bad, but Rather the Same? *Bioessays*, 42(7), 1900238.

77. **Fear of public speaking vs. fear of death**: Tuttar, J. (2018). Is Public Speaking Really More Feared Than Death? Retrieved from https://speakandconquer.com/is-public-speaking-really-more-feared-than-death/

78. **Chris Evans on his nerves**: Feinberg, S. (2020). 'Awards Chatter' Podcast - Chris Evans ('Defending Jacob'). Retrieved from https://www.hollywoodreporter.com/movies/movie-news/awards-chatter-podcast-chris-evans-defending-jacob-1295856/

79. **Adele on her stage fright**: Payne, C. (2011). Adele Talks Stage Fright:

'I Puke Quite a Lot'. Retrieved from https://www.billboard.com/music/music-news/adele-talks-stage-fright-i-puke-quite-a-lot-467590/

80. **Beyoncé and Sasha Fierce**: Touré. (2004). Beyonce Talks Fame, Relationships, Starting a Family, Becoming Sasha Fierce. Retrieved from https://www.rollingstone.com/music/music-features/beyonce-talks-fame-relationships-starting-a-family-becoming-sasha-fierce-111695/; **More on Sasha Fierce**: MacInnes, P. (2008). Beyoncé? We think you mean Sasha Fierce. Retrieved from https://www.theguardian.com/music/2008/oct/24/beyonce-sasha-fierce

81. **Beyoncé used the persona until well into her career**: McDonald, S. N. (2013). Finally free of Sasha Fierce, Beyoncé is a 'Grown Woman'. Retrieved from https://www.washingtonpost.com/blogs/she-the-people/wp/2013/12/28/finally-free-of-sasha-fierce-beyonce-is-a-grown-woman/

82. **CBT outperforming medications in treating anxiety**: This meta-analysis examined the results of several studies that included over 13,000 participants. Mayo-Wilson, E., Dias, S., Mavranezouli, I., Kew, K., Clark, D. M., Ades, A. E., & Pilling, S. (2014). Psychological and pharmacological interventions for social anxiety disorder in adults: A systematic review and network meta-analysis. *The Lancet Psychiatry*, 1(5), 368–376. https://doi.org/10.1016/S2215-0366(14)70329-3.

83. **The Dichotomy of Control**: Epictetus, ., & Higginson, T. W. (1955). *The Enchiridion*. Indianapolis: Bobbs-Merrill Educational Pub.

84. **"It is possible to commit no mistakes and still lose. That is not a weakness; that is life."**: Kemper, D. (Writer), & Scheerer, R. (Director). (1989, July 10). Peak Performance (Season 2, Episode 21) [TV series episode]. In R. Berman (Executive Producer), *Star Trek: The Next Generation*. Paramount Domestic Television.

Conclusion

85. **"Where does your mind end and the rest of the world begin?"**: Paul, A. M. (2021). *The Extended Mind: The Power of Thinking Outside the Brain.* Houghton Mifflin Harcourt.

86. **Most common regret on the deathbed**: Ware, B. (2011). *The Top Five Regrets of the Dying.* Hay House Inc.

About the Author

Christian Gilbert is a public speaker and educator. He is an Assistant Professor of Speech and Communication at the University of Hawaiʻi's Leeward Community College and recipient of 2014's *Outstanding Lecturer Award*. For over a decade, he has been training professionals in presentation skills, memory techniques, successful self-talk, nonverbal communication, and vital communication skills for the modern world. Aside from his expertise, Christian is known for his enthusiastic, entertaining, and approachable delivery style. He lives in Honolulu with his wife, Lucille, and dog, Tony.

To learn more about speaking events, trainings, or workshops with Christian visit www.ChristianGilbert.com.

Made in the USA
Columbia, SC
21 October 2022